LANDMARK COLLECTOR'S LIBRARY

THE SPIRIT OF LEEK: 1

THE 20TH CENTURY IN PHOTOGRAPHS

Cathryn Walton & Lindsey Porter

St Edward Street

Above: Job White's mill on Compton, lit up to show the Coronation decorations in 1953. See chapter 12, page 133, for more photographs of the town's Coronation celebrations

Across: Market day in The Market Place by the Challinor Fountain

THE SPIRIT OF
LEEK:1
THE 20TH CENTURY IN PHOTOGRAPHS

Cathryn Walton & Lindsey Porter

Published by

Landmark Publishing Ltd,

Waterloo House, 12 Compton, Ashbourne, Derbyshire DE6 1DA England
Tel: (01335) 347349 Fax: (01335) 347303
e-mail: landmark@clara.net www.landmarkpublishing.co.uk

1st edition

ISBN 1 901 522 86 5

British Library Cataloguing in Publication Data: a catalogue record for this book is
available from the British Library.

Printed by MPG Ltd, Bodmin, Cornwall
Designed by Ashley Emery
Cover by James Allsopp

Front cover: St Edward's Church in Edwardian times
Back cover Top: An outing awaits the train at Leek Railway Station
Back cover Middle: Derby Street, 1953, showing several properties now demolished
Back cover Bottom: Wendy Walton serves customers during the Pied Poudre Celebrations

Contents

	Foreword	6
1	Market Place	7
2	St Edward Street	31
3	Stockwell Street	41
4	Church Street	57
5	Overton Bank & Clerk Bank	66
6	Petty France	72
7	Derby Street	78
8	Pickwood Road	106
9	The Market Street Area	110
10	Cattle Market/Bus Station	114
11	The November Fair	126
12	1953 Coronation Arches	133
13	A Civic Year	144
14	Treading the Boards	149
15	Events	166
	Club Day 2000	187
	Index	190
	Subscribers List	191

Foreword

During the 19th century, Leek saw many changes as it developed as a textile town, with many new mills and streets. The 20th Century saw a rash of mill closures, several following a fire, and the demolition of many sub-standard houses under slum clearance schemes. Perhaps the majority of changes have been in the occupation of the shops. Here, both the names and the trades continually change.

Cathryn Walton has an incredible knowledge of the town centre shop keepers and their trades, as may be judged from the captions. This book is not just a book of photographs – a significant amount of historical detail comes across too, enhancing our knowledge of the shops and streets within which they are, or were to be found.

The heart of any town however is not its buildings but its people and both this book (and Volume 2, due in 2001) contain many photographs of townspeople, both young and old. We have tried to ensure that we included as many as possible and we hope that these bring as much enjoyment as the photographs of properties.

Some of the photographs included have been reproduced before, but we are confident that their inclusion here is justified, not only because of the additional information given, but because improved technology has meant that the quality of the reproduction is now so much better. The print run of this book is not great by printing standards and its price reflects both this and the time spent in ensuring that the print quality is as good as is possible. We hope that you are pleased with the results and that this book – and hopefully Volume 2 and our companion volume *Staffordshire Moorlands and the Churnet Valley* – find a treasured place on your bookshelf.

We wish to acknowledge the assistance we have received from lots of people. Thank you all very much. In particular, we wish to mention Kenneth Bowyer, Colin and Janet Broome, Margaret Hall, Marian Hulme, Pam Hurst, Leek and District Historical Society, Rowena Lovatt, John and Margaret Oliver, William Russell, Peggy Starling, Jim Stubbs, Basil Turner, Kathleen Turner, Wendy Walton, and John White. The authors and publisher acknowledge that a number of the photographs in this book are reproduced with the permission of the County Council and remain part of the Local History Collection housed in Leek Library. The assistance of the Leek Post and Times is particularly recognised, not only for some of the photographs which we know are theirs, but perhaps also for some used which are unattributed and may also be theirs. Perhaps the majority of the photographs are from the collection of CLM Porter and were taken by his maternal uncle, Arthur Goldstraw.

September 2000

The Challinor Fountain standing proudly at the bottom of the Market Place. Given to the town by William Challinor in 1876 it provided a focal point for Leek people. Townsfolk could stand and stare at its water display, small boys would frolic about its base and one enterprising trader, in Edwardian times, washed his fish in its waters!

An early view of the Market Place before the Buttermarket was built in 1897. The two small shops next to the Red Lion were occupied by George Allen, a saddler and harness maker, and by the Hassall family whose daughter Ellen traded as a milliner.

Woolworths has been established on the ground floor of the former Blacks Head since 1931, when it opened as a fancy bazaar. Built to a design by William Sugden in the late 1850's the new Blacks Head replaced an earlier inn of the same name. Boards on the front of the inn carry the name of Mr Lowe, a wine merchant, who is advertising Guinness and stout.

Some years later and the ornate branched lamp in the photograph above has been replaced by one in a plainer style. The stately Georgian house, home to the Cruso family, looks out over a deserted Market Place, stacked with stalls. Howe's grocers shop can be seen to the right as can a woollen drapers whose name appears to be Garside. Howe's was a family business, Thomas Howe passed on the business to his son Samuel.

This photograph taken before 1889 shows the old Bird in Hand, Redfern's baby linen shop, Warren's boot and shoe warehouse and William Henry Middleton's grocers shop. Sheets have been hung over the windows to protect goods from the sun. The shop between Redfern's and Warren's is probably that of John Adams who was a draper. The arch by the side of the shop led to Adam's Yard which held two houses.

The same shops in the 1960's. T.H. Booth, leather factors, now occupy the premises shared by Warren's shoe warehouse and Middleton's shop in the above photograph. In former years Thomas Henry Booth, tanner, currier and leather merchant, had a shop at 10, St. Edward Street and a tannery at 46, Ball Haye Road. Customers buying their nails from Booth's earlier this century would find they were wrapped in twists of paper taken from children's handwriting books! 21 and 22 Market Place have housed many shops over the years including Fitelson's Bazaar; today they are occupied by Oxfam.

    Next door is Beverley's wine and spirit merchants trading from the shop which was once John Adams drapers shop. Another charity shop has taken over this building, namely Imperial Cancer Research.

The steps of the Challinor Fountain providing a welcome resting place for two weary workmen.

Icicles adorn the fountain on a snowy winter day.

A busy Market Day in the years after 1897, the Buttermarket has been built and the building which we now know as Foxlowe is still a private house. On the right is Hiltons Booteries, standing between the Angel and Star Tea Co. The Red Lion, formerly Leek Old Hall, presents a pleasant face to this bustling scene. Bradley's clothiers shop projects into the Market Place on the top left of the photograph.

Market Day in the early 1900s. Freeman, Hardy and Willis and Slater's Supply Stores can be seen to the left of this photograph. They are trading from the shops which later became Booth's leather shop and is now Oxfam.

This and the adjacent photograph are from a group several of which are dated from the middle of the 1890s. It shows a typical market day scene. Behind the lamp post can be seen the sign of the Singer sewing machine shop which traded here for many years.

Plaid shawls predominate in this Victorian photograph of Market Day shoppers.

Whatever is being sold on this market stall seems to be attracting more men than women. An unusual occurrence on Market Day.

Ladies wrapped up warmly in shawls and cloaks, hats firmly on their heads, baskets safely clutched in their hands, stare quizzically at a pedlar as he opens his box of wares.

Jumbled, higgledy-piggledy, together are ramshackle cages containing scrawny chickens and ducks, awaiting their fate on Market day. Wooden baskets, crates and boxes are stacked erratically on the cobbles and the whole market has a rakish appearance. A wonderful photograph full of character.

Stately ladies survey the scene somewhat hesitatingly. Are they really going to mingle with the other shoppers?

Meeting old friends, catching up with local news and exchanging a friendly greeting has always been a feature of Market Day. We still do it today but not usually with dead birds under our arms!

Edwin Trafford first traded as a butcher in Stanley Street but was established at 16, Market Place from at least 1904. These premises are now part of Style Sports.

An errand boy in his white apron waits for his orders, rabbits in a cage behind him wait to be sold. An old gas lamp can be seen to the left of the Challinor fountain.

Cheeses stacked on the pavement outside William Spearing's shop at 24 and 25, Market Place. Spearings also had premises at 3, Church Street. Fred Spearing ran a grocers shop at 13, Stockwell Street in later years.

A horse drawn snow plough clears the Market Place in this evocative photograph recalling winters past.

Men, women, children, horses, cart, trestles, canopies, stalls and shops combine to paint a picture of another bustling Market Day in the early years of the century. Spearings is still trading on the left, galvanised pails hang in a row outside the shop next door and an advertisement for Thorley's cakes can be seen nearby.

Leek's first Public Hall stood at the south end of the Market Place in front of the shops now occupied by Bell's Shoes and Style Sports. It was erected in 1806 on the site of the Market Cross which was moved to Cornhill on the Cheddleton Road. The hall was open to the elements on the ground floor when it was first built, but was later enclosed due to meetings of the wrong sort taking place its its dark corners. It provided a newsroom, a savings bank and cells for felons. No longer adequate for the town's needs it was sold for £85 to Joseph Flower in 1872. Mr Flower used the stone to built Portland House which once stood in Rosebank Street.

Micah Carding traded as a painter, plumber and glazier at 2 and 3 Market Place for many years. Carding's shop was part of the former Cock Inn, a flourishing establishment in the 18th century, able to provide numerous beds for weary travellers and several private parlours for exclusive use. In 1731 John Naden spent his last night in the cellars of the Cock before he was hung on Gun and his corpse gibbeted there. In later years part of these premises were used as a bank. In 1864 the inn was purchased by the Leek Improvement Commissioners who were considering building a new Town Hall and a covered market on the site. At this time the old inn had been divided into two shops, (pictured above) a doctors surgery, a blacksmith's shop, a cottage and several storerooms. The shops faced the Market Place but the other premises fronted Stockwell Street.

This large property was demolished and new premises built which house the Tourist Information Centre and council offices.

The Earl of Shrewsbury's coach waits patiently for a dog to cross over the cobbles in 1893. Between Carding's and the Red Lion are Henry Ellerton's drapers shop and George Lee Baskerville's watch and clock makers shop. Just visible on the left is the sign over Nathan Gosling's shop. He was a clothier and tailor.

The Earl sold the horses in October 1893. Was this a photo of his last coach service between Alton Towers and Buxton?

Star Tea Co. Ltd or Star Supply Store traded at 9, Market Place during the first half of the century. Their shop window is packed with goods of every sort, They sold pears, peaches, tomatoes, sweets, margarine and 'pure lard'. Their cooked meats are advertised as the best in town, you could choose from several blends of tea including Ceylon and Darjeeling and butter could be bought for 1/6d per pound. Well remembered brands such as 'Rinso' are represented and you could join their Christmas Club which would give you 2/- to the pound. Occupying a prime position, Star Tea Co. was a truly one stop shop, a boon to the people of Leek before giant supermarkets forced shoppers to the outskirts of the town. This shop later became Fred Attaway's outfitters and from the 1960's to 1994 was occupied by Playland; it is now part of Argos.

Another celebratory gathering in the Market Place, possibly a Royal occasion as many flags are fluttering from the buildings. The windows of the house which we now know as Foxlowe are open as people crane out to watch the proceedings. Small boys dangle precariously from on top of the archway to the right of the house and the crowds have spilled from the pavement on to the cobbles. Robert West, a clockmaker, is still trading in the building at the north west corner of the Market Place. He erected the clock seen on this building in 1883. Robert West, who hailed from Bolton, had previously traded from a shop at 9, Stockwell Street.

(above right) Another gathering in the Market Place, Bunting is strung between the buildings and flags fly from every available window.

(right) Club Day 1907.
Demure young ladies sing decorously, accompanied by clarinets, cornets and conspicuous brass instruments.

Leek Church Schools gathered in the Market Place in July 1907. In a lofty position is the conductor on his platform surrounded by a multitude of hats. In the background are the Red Lion, the Buttermarket and Star Supply Store.

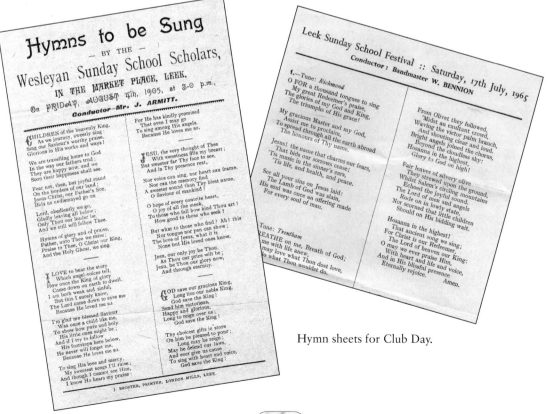

Hymn sheets for Club Day.

Another view of the buildings at the top of the Market Place. Bradley's was very popular with Leek children who were presented with a ruler if they went into the shop and recited this rhyme.

> *Fear not, fear not, my darling wife,*
> *A Bradley's shirt has saved my life.*
> *It did not tear or let me down,*
> *Although it cost but half-a-crown.*

The building with the single column of three windows, squashed into the corner, next to Bradley's was the shop of William Birch, a clog maker.

What are little boys made of? Bashful smiles, cheeky grins, resignation, boredom and bravado feature on these faces of boys taking part in Club Day c.1930. After all what young boy wants to be dressed in his best and walk around with girls!

Girls from St. John's Sunday School hold on to their ribbons as they assemble in the Market Place in the 1940s.

Sunday School teachers, banner bearers and pupils from St.Luke's captured on film in the mid 1950s.

With well scrubbed knees, slicked down hair and beaming smiles these young lads prepare to sing lustily in the Market Place c.1958.

A photograph taken before 1940 features an unknown group of girls outside Star Supply Stores. This shop is now part of Argos. Note the ladies sitting on the first floor window sill!

St. Luke's Sunday School passing the Red Lion as they process out of the Market Place in the mid 1970s.

Club Day in the 1970s. The Market Place is not nearly as crowded as it was in former years and there is definitely not so many hats!

Club Day in the Market Place c.1992.
Sunday School pupils and Scouts still gather in the Market Place for this traditional event. The Market Place retains it's cobbled appearance, the Buttermarket is the same, the shop buildings survive, although they have changed hands many times, but the Red Lion has a dilapidated and neglected appearance.

A veritable sea of hats as officials, dignitaries and townsfolk gather at the south end of the Market Place to witness the proclamation of King George V in 1910. Firemen in their best brass helmets hold back the crowd on what is obviously Market Day. The Challinor fountain is almost hidden by the mass of people.

A different perspective of the same occasion. The shops in the background can be identified as Brooks' Boot Factors and Samuel Heath's, saddler and harness makers. Brook's is now Bells Shoes and Mr. Heath's saddlers shop is the sports shop of Gary Plant and his wife Diane.

The George Hotel
LEEK.

THE RECOGNISED FAMILY, COMMERCIAL AND MOTORISTS' HOTEL.

Entirely free from Brewers or Spirit Merchants.

FIFTEEN BEDROOMS.
Stabling for 20 horses.

EXCELLENT MOTOR ACCOMMODATION.

This Hotel is most conveniently situated for all the neighbouring resorts.—RUDYARD LAKE,

The George Hotel stood on the corner of Church Street and St. Edward Street, opposite The Swan. Built in the 1760s it was both a coaching inn and posting house, where horses were kept as relays for post or travellers. Coaches from London to Manchester called at The George daily towards the end of the 18th century. Until it was demolished in 1972, the George Hotel continued to provide accommodation and meals as well as offering hospitality for meetings of all kinds. Many Leek people will remember the upper room at the hotel which, during the sixties, was used for discos and as a venue for the Folk Club and the Beat Club. In 1963, The George always provided a live group and top records on Sundays and Tuesdays.

A view of St. Edward Street showing its pleasant aspect with wide, spacious pavements and fine buildings. Formerly known as Spout Street it is one of Leek's oldest thoroughfares and had become the town's main residential streets by the early 19th century. This lower end of the street was widened and cleared in the 1890s and in 1896 the Unicorn Inn was set back and rebuilt, opening up the vista of the street. Victoria Buildings to the left were erected in 1897.

The Trades Demonstration in June 1907 surges down St. Edward Street, passing in front of Victoria Buildings before wheeling right into Broad Street. Victoria Buildings with their mock Tudor frontage, provide an impressive 'gateway' into this wide, pleasant street with its interesting architecture.

Flags fly as the parade marking the marriage of Princess Mary to the Duke of Teck progresses up St. Edward Street in July 1893. People watch from a window by The Bull's Head while across the road residents lean out of the windows of William Allen's house at 50, St. Edward Street. William Allen was a solicitor working for the firm of Hacker and Allen whose offices were next door.

William Allen, who married Eliza Clowes in 1852, had fourteen children, though all did not survive to adulthood. Five of these children were born in the large, rambling house pictured here, identified by the sign for Strangmans Walks on the side of the property. Strangmans Walks was a small passageway, just ten feet wide. It was later widened and extended becoming the Strangman Street which we know today.

Thomas Wardle, the famous Leek dyer, lived next door to the Allen's at 54, with his wife, Elizabeth, and his large family. In common with most of the occupiers of the large houses in St. Edward Street at this time, the Wardle family employed several servants, including two housemaids. Elizabeth Wardle's School of Embroidery and the headquarters of the Leek Embroidery Society operated from the little shop situated just below their house.

A picturesque snow scene in the street. The house with the steps leading to the front door was once the home of Stephen Goodwin, silk manufacturer. Britannia Mill, the factory of Messrs. Goodwin and Tatton, and situated at the top of West Street, was destroyed by fire during World War II. Later occupiers of this house at 47, St. Edward Street were medical men. Doctor Edgar Somerville, physician and surgeon, practised here for many years, before taking Dr. Hallowes as his partner. Many people will remember Doctor Pepperdine when he lived at this house. In recent memory Doctors Johnson, Saddler and Richardson had their surgery here and Bernard Broadhurst's dental practice operated at this property. Currently the house is used by yet another medical man, namely P. Phillips, dental surgeon.

31, St. Edward Street. The advertisements on the windows of these premises indicate that this was an establishment providing liquid refreshment. The Grapes public house traded here for many years in competition with at least eight other establishments in St. Edward Street; perhaps the reason for its closure in the early 1900s. After The Grapes closed, Nellie and Lizzie Maycock had a toy shop here, followed by Margaret Whitehead who ran a millinery shop. Mr. Tatler, the master tailor, made fine suits here, his customers choosing material from bound swatches of diverse cloth. After Mr. Tatler retired, Fine Sounds, selling sheet music and musical instruments, took over the shop. Today it is part of Leek Pet and Fishing Centre.

Maskery's confectionery shop was established in 1796, the proprietor at the time being Francis Maskery. The business operated from 58, St. Edward Street for many years before expanding to include the shop next door. Maskery's bakers and confectioners are remembered with great affection by many Leek people, not least for the succulent fingers of 'Leek' gingerbread, bath buns and tasty wakes cakes which could be bought there. Maskery's had a cafe on the first floor. It was a long, low room with an uneven wooden floor, which creaked and groaned when walked upon.

Shirley's Buildings, 17, St. Edward Street

This fine building on the corner of Sheepmarket dated 1875 was still being built in 1881 for Mr. Shirley, a cheese factor and seedsman. Designed by Larner Sugden in the Arts and Craft style it bristles with interesting decorative features. A glance upwards, next time you walk past, will reveal massive chimney stacks, carved stonework, pillars, a round window, gables and to top it all a lion who gazes impassively over the busy street scene. As the shop sign indicates, E. Green traded here; he is listed as a provision dealer in the directory of 1892. The cheeses stacked on the pavement and the hams hanging temptingly outside his shop may make our mouths water, even as we reflect on the lack of refrigeration in those days! The whole carcasses seemingly fixed to the shop frontage appear strange by todays standards. We are used to our meat neatly packaged and far removed from its source.

Boots Cash Chemist later traded from this shop. Recently it has been used as an Indian restaurant called Al Minar and now Shapla Tandoori.

On the opposite corner to the Indian restaurant is Pickford's grocers shop. These premises were built in 1907 for Mr. Ernie Green who kept the shop across the road. George Henry Pickford worked for Mr. Green and in time took over the shop. Percy Pickford, his son, carried on the business after his father's death and until recently Kevin

Pickford, Percy's son, ran the business with his wife Stella. Truly a long established family business which has closed this year. The shop next to Pickford's was once Pegg's greengrocers, then a bookshop and now sells fabric. The next three properties were demolished to make way for the new General Post Office which opened in 1964. Sam Godwin had a butcher's shop at 30, St Edward Street from at least 1908. Salter and Salter, boot manufacturers traded from 32, St. Edward Street for many years.

This street scene from the 1960s shows Westminster Bank on the corner of High Street with the Wilkes' Head public house next door. Above the entrance to Court No.2 is Stannard's shoe shop followed by Norman Ash's jewellery shop. Parr's bank was built on the site of the old Plough Inn in 1885. This was a Warrington based business and not surprisingly the bank in Leek was built to a design by W. Owen of Warrington. By 1923, the bank had become the Westminster Bank Ltd. The bank on this site closed in 1970 and the premises are now used by Leek Volunteer Bureau.

The Wilkes Head is one of only five inns in Britain named after the political reformer. Parker's brewery which provided the beer for this pub was taken over by Ind Coope. Stannard's shoe shop is now the home of the John Worthy Gallery while Norman Ash's shop is occupied by Go-Go Designs.

Taken from St Edward Street is this scene of Sheep Market. Home Aids occupies the site of the old Cheshire Cheese Inn. In Edwardian days Ted Gee's chip shop stood here. His son, Fred, converted it to a chemists, later selling out to Timothy Whites. Many people will remember Norman Ash's jeweller's shop being here.

Leek's first purpose built Post Office stood on the corner of Strangman Street and St.Edward Street.

This interesting building opened in or shortly after 1905; with its decorative brickwork and elegant stonework this Post Office was certainly more pleasing to the eye than its replacement further up the street. A new telephone exchange opened in the Post Office yard in 1928. In 1968, a subscriber trunk dialling exchange was built on the site of this old Post Office.

The large town houses on the right of this photograph were once the homes of Leek's wealthier residents. Most of the town's silk manufacturers made their homes in this wide, leafy, pleasant street. The Sleighs, Wardle's, Challinor's, Ward's, Goodwin's and the Russell's all lived in this street at some time. Cheek by jowl with Leek's elite lived the workers whom they employed in their factories. In the court off St.Edward Street, next to Thomas Wardle's house, were 10 houses crammed full of families who shared lavatories and bedrooms. The occupants of these houses were silk winders, piecers, dyers, porters, brickmakers, an unemployed cotton spinner and a 15 year old unemployed silk helper!

The street decorated ready for the coronation festivities in 1911. The young lady in the pushchair gazes at the fluttering flags while the gentleman in the bowler hat seems to be studying his hand! Ladies stroll serenely, errand boys pause pensively while delivering bread and carrier's carts clatter over the cobbles. Gas lamps guard the wide pavements and railings protect the fronts of the "gentlemens' residences" to the left of the street.

During the 1920s, Leek staged a carnival each year; it was a charitable enterprise with the proceeds being donated to the Leek Cottage Hospital. Here the carnival floats parade along St. Edward Street as crowds gather on the pavement to watch. The aeroplane was the float of W. Turner, builders, who entered a float every year. This aeroplane had a propeller which turned and hinged wings, which had to be folded when the float negotiated the street corners!

A different parade in the street shows St. Mary's Scout and Guide Band in 1978. Spectators still stand on the pavement, but are not nearly as numerous as the crowds in the photograph above. The parade in the 1920s, however, was not competing with televised sport.

The only shop which has not changed hands is that of Small's Vac Centre. G. Davies's shop is now Simpson's and the shop below is now New Leek Curry House. 43. St. Edward Street, above the arch, is now the offices of Hulme Upright and Partners, architects.

William Fallon's shop in St. Edward Street was demolished when the High Street was cut through. Hanging outside the shop are hens, ducks, geese and a large deer. Fallon's also sold fruit and fish. At other times they had shops in Stockwell Street and Derby Street.

On the right is the property which became the Westminster bank. After Fallon's was demolished it became the property on the corner of St. Edward Street and High Street.

65, St. Edward Street. Pictured here is Joseph Ratcliffe & Sons plumber's shop. Although the decal on the building informs us that the firm was established in 1800 it only traded from this address in St. Edward Street for some time in the early 1900s. High on the building to the left of this shop could be seen a large tobacco pipe affixed to the wall. Indeed this shop at 63, St. Edward street was a tobacconist's for many years in the second half of the 19th century. In 1861 George Spilsbury ran the tobacconist's shop there, living on the premises with his wife, Mary, their four young children and a servant.

Stockwell Street before the advent of the motor car. Hooves strike on the cobblestones as a cart lumbers up the street towards the Market Place. Carts of all shapes and sizes line the street awaiting goods to transport around the town and to neighbouring villages. The right hand side of the street remains unchanged. Ford House and the gable end of Stockwell Cottage can be seen in the distance.

Today we know 1 and 3 Stockwell street as the White Hart Craft Studio, in earlier years two bow windows fronted this property. It was J.E. Haworth who opened the White Hart Restaurant here; he used to keep the Temperance Hotel at the former Field House, which is now the National Reserve Club. The ladies in their neat black and white uniforms, standing outside the restaurant would serve you hot and cold luncheons in the dining rooms or tea rooms. Haworths were also bakers, confectioners and caterers. Charlie Haworth replaced the bow windows with plate glass ones, which did not protrude into the street and also added a middle window. Before the Haworth's took over these premises they had been occupied by Selina Bowcock, a baker and confectioner and by Gaddum's, silk merchants.

The old bow window of Haworth's can be seen in this early photograph of a leisurely and leafy Stockwell Street Next to it is 5, Stockwell Street which used to be the home of Miss Mary Hawksworth, a dressmaker and later of Sidney Mountcastle Phillips. This house had a large garden at the rear. On the opposite side of the street, below the gas lamp is 10, Stockwell Street. This large house was originally the home of Thomas Walthall, a lawyer. In the 20th century it has housed members of the Flint family, descendants of Charles Flint, a Leek doctor, who lived here long ago. Mrs Edward Challinor lived here in 1912, but in more recent years it will be recalled as being the dental surgery of Mr. Starkie, the Moorlands Training Centre and Leek College Training Centre.

The house on the right of this photograph, next to Cruso's Yard, was demolished some years ago.

Cruso's yard containing the former stables belonging to the Cruso House at the top of the Market Place, which we now know as Foxlowe. Nine houses stood in this yard whose official address was Court No.1, Stockwell Street.

This early photograph clearly shows Leek Bank at 7, Stockwell Street. This bank was opened by Francis William Jennings in 1857. He sold the bank to Parr's Banking Co. Ltd; in 1885 Parr's Bank moved into premises in St. Edward Street. The Nicholson Institute has not been built and a cottage projects on to the pavement below Greystones

11 and 13, Stockwell Street have been demolished for many year, next to them was Court No. 3 containing three houses. This Court was known as Cavendish Square. In this photograph, taken in the 1960s we can see Grosvenor's antiques shop and Fred Spearing, family grocer's. Spearing had been at this shop for many years but in the early 1900s it was occupied by James Fisher, nurseryman and seedsman. 11, Stockwell Street was once the refreshment rooms of Thomas Rendall.

Gas lamps, cobbles and shady trees present a pleasant prospect in this view, taken some time after 1937. In the left foreground are the former offices of the Leek and Moorlands Permanent Benefit Building Society at 15, Stockwell Street. This Building Society had been established at 1, Stockwell Street in 1856. These new offices were built at 15, Stockwell Street in 1894-5, designed by J.T. Brearley. Thomas Brearley was the secretary of the Leek and Moorlands Building Society for many years. This property later housed the offices of the Royal Insurance Society and is now the headquarters of Leek Town Council. Many people will remember kindly Mr. Hilton who had his dental surgery on the upper floor of this building.

The former Stockwell House situated between the old Buiding Society Offices at 15, Stockwell Street and Greystones. This imposing building had a large garden at the rear. It was the home of the Nicholson Family of Brough, Nicholson and Hall, who had moved here from Greystones. Joshua and Ellen Nicholson lived at Stockwell House with their children and servants. By 1932 it was the home of Colonel Arthur Falkner Nicholson. and was demolished before 1936.

Part of the pleasure garden behind the former Stockwell House.

New Stockwell House, built 1936/7 on the site of the old Stockwell House. New Stockwell House was the headquarters of the Leek and Moorlands Building Society.

The coronation procession parades past Ford House in 1911. In the first row are Anthony Ward, Sir A Nicholson, Hugh Richard Sleigh and William Hassal. In the next row are H. Henshaw, William Allen, O.H.Bishton (Chairman of Leek Urban District Council) and Thomas Mason (Vice Chairman).

The building at the top of Stockwell Street which was used as Leek's fire station from 1870. This old property was once part of the Cock Inn, which stood on the corner of the Market Place and Stockwell Street. The large house in the centre is 10, Stockwell Street, still in use as a private house at this time. Between this house and the fire station buildings is a small shop which was occupied by the Fallon family (see below).

This is John Fallon's shop at 8, Stockwell Street, where he traded as a fishmonger and poulterer. John Fallon had moved to another shop in Derby Street by 1904. His son William, had a shop in St. Edward Street at this time. William's shop was near to the Globe Inn, which was pulled down to make way for the entrance to High Street (see page 40).

Shrouded in sheeting and surrounded by scaffolding the Nicholson Institute undergoes neccesary repairs in the summer of 2000.

A cow strolls, slowly, past the entrance to the Nicholson Institute. This Queen Anne style building, of brick with stone dressings, was designed by William Sugden. It was presented to the town by Joshua Nicholson and opened in 1884. The library contained over 6,000 books and was open to all adults living within 6 miles of Leek. The Nicholson Institute also contained a museum and three picture galleries.

The late 17th century Greystones presents a timeless face to both old and modern Stockwell Street. The cottage next to Greystones has long gone as have the cobblestones.The railings on the wall opposite have been replaced with a hedge but little else seems to have changed. Greystones once had a garden at the rear with views over Hillswood and Gun. Sunflowers and hollyhocks blossomed in this quaint garden which was lost when the Nicholson Institute was built. Joshua Nicholson lived at this house before he moved next door to Stockwell House. For many years Henry Salt, who was first a cashier and eventually a director of Brough, Nicholson and Hall, lived here. Greystones is now the award winning tea rooms of Mr and Mrs Warrilow.

Looking out of the Nicholson
Institute gates on to a snow covered
Market Street.

The Nicholson Institute seen
through the arch erected in Market
Street to celebrate the opening of
the Leek School of Art. The notices
on each side of the arch read
Prosperity to the Leek School of Art
and *If a good man thrives all thrive
with him.*

Boys of St. Edward's Scout Troop look happy and proud as they march past the gate posts of the Nicholson Institute in 1911. They were taking part in the coronation festival parade. Small boys look on, enviously, from their vantage point on top of the wall outside Greystones.

The banner of West Street Wesleyan Sunday School makes its way down Stockwell Street in the same parade.

Stockwell Street almost hidden by the mass of people gathered to watch the parade. Here the Boys Brigade take centre stage.

The Majestic Cinema in Union Street, conjures up happy memories for Leek children, who spent many enjoyable hours inside. The Majestic occupied the former Temperance Hall and opened as a cinema in the early 1920s. It was gutted by fire in 1961 and was demolished soon afterwards.

A crowd of children gathered outside the Majestic Cinema. The boys grin, engagingly at the front, while the girls smile, happily behind them. Whether they were waiting to go in, or had just come out, is not known.

In the centre left of this photograph are 29 and 31 Stockwell Street, just below the gates of the Nicholson Institute. Both of these houses seem to have been connected with the medical profession through the years. 29 has housed Thomas Warrington, a physician, D. Bulbeck, a chiropodist and will be remembered as the home of Nurse Steele, a midwife, who delivered many of Leek's babies, mostly in their own homes. 31 was once occupied by Peter Bluett, a physician and surgeon, and is now the dental surgery of Mr. A Worth.

Further down the street on the corner, opposite the Union (now Benks) is 41, Stockwell Street. Now the Bolka Spice Restaurant, in former years it was a shop and confectioners.

57 and 59, Stockwell Street in the early 1900's was occupied by Peter Rayner, railway parcel agent and Sutton and Co, carriers. Sutton's cart bears the advertisement *parcels and goods collected and delivered to all parts of the world*. To the right of Rayner's are the premises of H Brough and Son, box manufacturer's, whose address was 1 and 2 Garden Bank, Stockwell Street. This building has been demolished but the property occupied by Rayner's still stands and is now Blakemore and Chell's showroom.

These houses in Union Street, locally called "Brickbank" have disappeared with the passing of time. Prestigeous new college buildings have replaced some of these dwellings. The road is now smooth and tarmaced and leads to a neatly laid out car park at the bottom of Brough Park.

Sheep shuffle through the snow in this evocative picture of former days in Stockwell Street. The shop on the corner with Bath Street will be remembered as the old fashioned, delightfully jumbled shop of Miss Goodwin, who sold sweets and patent remedies. It is now an off-licence store. Doctor Godwin used to live in one of the large houses on the right of this photograph.

This building, which stood just above the Cottage Hospital, has been demolished.

James Alsop died in 1868 and his widow Adelina Alsop built the Leek Memorial Cottage Hospital in memory of her husband. The hospital was designed by William Sugden and opened in 1870. When the hospital first opened it had two wards with beds for four men and three women, two cots and two private wards containing one bed each. This photograph was taken before 1909.

The Cottage Hospital, as it was always known by Leek people, was extended in 1909 as this photograph shows. The new wing was designed by W. Sugden & Co. Part of the cost was raised by public subscription and part funded by a legacy from Elizabeth Flint.

Stockwell Street and the junction with Buxton Road. Times have changed since this photograph was taken, the Cottage Hospital has closed and has been converted into flats and a new medical centre has been built on the opposite corner.

Boxing Day 1983 and the North Staffordshire Hunt ride past Stockwell House after assembling in the Market Place.

Church Street, lavishly adorned with foliage and flags, on a hot summer's day in June 1887. Queen Victoria's Golden Jubilee was celebrated throughout the town with parades, feasts, sports, dancing, fireworks, bonfires and much merriment.

Here a group of people are pictured outside the Conservative Club. This Tudor style building was erected in 1887 on the site of the former Crown Inn, which was pulled down in 1886. The Conservative Club, founded in 1882, formerly met in the Union Buildings in Market Street. Opened on 12 April 1887, by Mr Harry Davenport MP, the Conservative Club contained a reading room and a "double American bowling alley". Upstairs were two billiard rooms, two smoking or card rooms and a dining room.

The south side of Church Street was demolished in 1972 in order to widen the road and to improve the junction with St. Edward Street.

This arch in Stockwell Street was erected to celebrate the visit of the Duke and Duchess of York on 28th July 1900. This unusual view shows the side of West's shop which faced Stockwell Street. The other side stretched down Church Street opposite the shops and vicarage. Their view of the town was much improved when this property was demolished (see page 60).

A lovely view of the picturesque, ivy clad, Parker House in Church Street, before it was converted into shops. It abuts on to the house now known as Foxlowe, which is in the Market Place. Railings, which can be seen in front of Foxlowe, have long since disappeared.

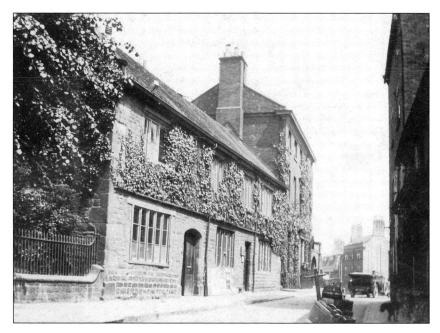

A view of the old, narrow, Church Street circa 1920. Wooden pails and other implements are stacked on the roadway. The houses on the left are 2 and 4 Church Street next to the vicarage. In the years before 1919 Mr Arthur Parker, land agent and surveyor occupied 4, Church Street, which was the estate office of the Earl of Macclesfield. (Thomas Parker, who became the 1st Earl of Macclesfield was born in these premises in 1666). In 1916 George Hardy, an electrician traded from this property. For many years 4, Church Street has been known as Bill's store, fondly known as "Bill the Bandit".

2, Church Street was converted into two shops, which have changed hands and trades, often, over the years. In 1932 and 1940 John Joseph Curtis was a cabinet maker at number 2. Mrs Cumberlidge has sold hats for many years in the Market Place and the shop next door has seen many tenants having traded as a ladies clothes shop, a music shop and a garden shop, to name but a few.

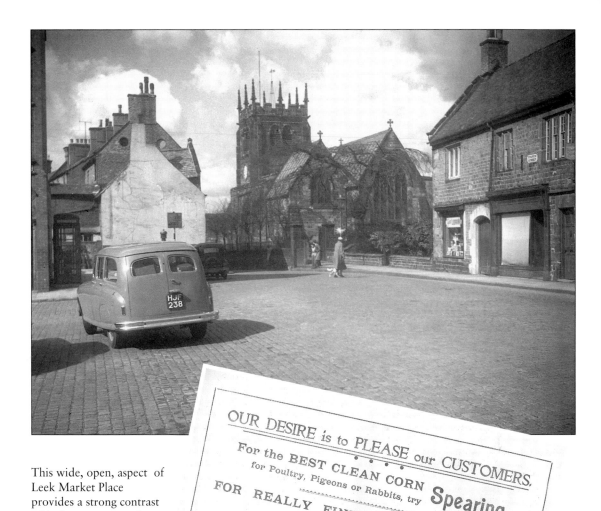

This wide, open, aspect of Leek Market Place provides a strong contrast with the entrance to the relatively dark and narrow Church Street. This photograph was obviously taken after 1930, when the group of buildings on the corner of the Market Place and Church Street had been demolished. Some of these interesting old buildings spanned both Church Street and the Market Place. The properties in Church Street which were pulled down included 3 and 5 Church Street and the lodging house which stood behind them. William Spearing had traded as a corn merchant and provision dealer from 3 Church Street and Tommy Moreton had been a baker and confectioner at number 5. A passageway led from the street to Mrs. Dudgeon's lodging house, fondly known as the Hotel Duggan. In the last years of the 19th century itinerant travellers, of diverse trades could be sure of a night in an establishment which was always spotlessly clean. Mrs Duggan's also ran a rag and bone emporium where she traded in old clothes and rabbit skins. In the years before 1930 Mrs. Skarratt ran this "common lodging house" in Church Street.

The vicarage and the two adjacent properties, 2 and 4 Church Street, had a most pleasant view of the Market Place, after the properties opposite them disappeared. They now appear to be more of the Market Place than Church Street.

The exposed gable end of 7 Church Street, giving a rather dingy and dilapidated appearance to the start of the street in the 1960's. This small property has been both a private house and a shop over the years.

Grocers, tailors, saddlers and butchers have traded from this shop. In 1912 Samuel Birch worked as a hairdresser here.

Narrow Church Street with a pavement only on the south side. At one time four public houses in Church Street did brisk business with Leek's thirsty inhabitants. The building with the arched doorway and the sign is the Golden Lion, on the other side of the archway, next to the Golden Lion stood the King William IV. A little further along Church Street was the Crown and at the end of the street stood the George.

The Golden Lion Inn at 9 Church Street is still remembered by many Leek people. This old established inn was a busy drinking establishment as long ago as 1829. At that time it boasted a bar and five rooms on the ground floor, a brewhouse and eleven bedrooms. In the large yard behind the Inn had stabling for forty horses and there were five warehouses. One of these warehouses was occupied as a dwelling house and another was used as a slaughter house.

Next to the Golden Lion, separated by an archway, stood this property which was formerly the King William IV. In 1908 it was still in use as a hostelry, but in 1912 was occupied by John Steele, a scale maker, and Margaret Steele, a midwife.

13, Church Street was the "pop shop" or pawnbroker's business of Ernest Carter who had traded here from at least 1932. Before Ernie Carter, the shop was the business of Mr. William Taylor Walker who had another pawnbroker's shop in Russell Street. In the late 19th and early 20th century this shop was occupied by Sarah Howes, a grocer.

15, Church Street, another old property with a new shop front. For many years this was the millinery shop of Hannah and Sarah Garner. In living memory it has been the confectionery shop of Mr. Granville Wragg, the tobacconist shop of Doris Goodwin and later of Mr. C Bowling.

The Conservative Club can be seen at 17, Church Street next to number 19, which bears the name of Mrs. Cumberlidge who kept a hat shop here. This property had been the home of milliners for some years. Mrs Cumberlidge had taken over from Mrs. Barlow, who was the successor of Mrs. Bowyer. Before this succession of ladies who sold hats, it was the private house of Mrs. Murfin. In the early years of the 20th century it was the shop of Henry Cosgrove, a watchmaker. He had traded here for many years.

A view of the lower end of Church Street showing the Conservative Club, Cumberlidge's Hat shop and the George Hotel. Yet another place for liquid refreshment can be seen, namely The Swan. Note the absence of the attractive black and white frontage and the pleasant wide pavement, which we see today.

On St. George's Day in 1950, Scouts and Guides parade past the Golden Lion in Church Street. Taking the salute, outside the vicarage, are Arthur Bloor, the Scout Divisional Commissioner and Muriel Carr, the Guides Divisional Commissioner.

St. George's Day 1993 and the 2nd Leek Scout band lead the parade into Church Street. The Swan has had a facelift, the pavements are wider and the junction with St. Edward Street is much improved.

A gas lamp stands guard, carts rumble over the cobbles, others are lined up under the church wall and ladies, dressed in their best, saunter along the pavement below Overton Bank. Apart from the loss of the cobbles and the gain of a continuous traffic flow, little has changed. The trees in front of the Old Church have grown, hiding the view from passers-by, but the properties along Clerk Bank are much the same. The property with the open blind is 1, Clerk Bank which now trades as Hopwood, Benyon, Willot and Crew, an antiques shop. Around the turn of the century George Metcalfe kept this shop. He was followed by William Pickford and then by Enoch Harrison, who had a butcher's shop here in 1904. Older inhabitants of the town may remember the Warrington family who traded here for over 20 years. Large crowds gathered outside on the day of Edward Warrington's funeral as his coffin was taken from this house to his final resting place.

Scouts in their early uniforms and gentlemen in straw boaters pass beneath the throngs of people lining Overton Bank to watch the Sunday School Festival of 1910. The large house on the left, now called Overton Bank House, may have been the home of George Davenport, silk manufacturer and John Pomeroy Hitchcock who owned an iron and brass foundry on Newcastle Road.

West Street Sunday School scholars head fo the Market Place on Club Day 1910.

The cottages on Clerk Bank still look much the same as does the corner of the Swan and the trees on Overton Bank. However the scene at the top of Mill Street and West Street are vastly different. Missing are the toilets at the top of Mill street, not yet built and the Factory of Stephen Goodwin and Tatton Ltd. which was destroyed by fire during the 1940s.

Market Day in Leek as drovers and cattle wend their weary way up Mill Street to reach the Cattle Market. The cows, not being conversant with the Highway Code, did not always keep to the road and would often run down entries and become trapped in backyards. Children delighted in the mayhem which followed as the animals were chased back into the road!

The property on the left has been demolished but the house standing next to it is Bank House or Clerk Bank House which has recently been repainted in an authentic blue shade. Bank House has been home to William Young, Thomas Wardle (not Sir Thomas) and Ralph de Tunstall Sneyd. Doctors Depree and Mansbridge practised here and Norman Smith ran an undertakers business from this property. In recent years it has been home to Inghams Architects and is now divided between Christopher Taylor Design and Roger Brooks, a solicitor. To the right is Salt's builders yard on Overton Bank.

Further along Clerk Bank we reach Mount Pleasant House and Mount Pleasant Wesleyan Methodist Chapel with its graveyard. Mount Pleasant House has been home to many people including George Vernon Myatt, Miss Bolton, Samuel Price and Hector McIntyre who was a Veterinary Surgeon. Mount Pleasant Chapel was demolished in 1980 and Beth Johnson sheltered housing flats were built on the site. The former graveyard is now a pleasant garden, several graves remain on site including that of John Mien, a French prisoner of war, and his descendants.

The lodge to Brow Hill House which stood opposite to the photograph above. This house was home to generations of the Myatt family after Thomas Myatt bought the house from Henry Brunt for £1650 in 1883. The Town Council bought the house and grounds in 1959 intending to convert it into flats but demolished it after deciding that it could not be economically brought into use. Council housing has been built on the site of the house and its grounds.

The Quaker cottages on Overton bank next to the Meeting House of the Society of Friends. The four cottages are numbered 9 to 12 and are comparatively small inside. In the late 19th Century Daniel Tipper, a shoemaker lived at number 10 with his wife, three grown up daughters, a young son and a granddaughter! To the right of the cottages was the entrance to Court No. 2, Overton Bank. This photograph, taken in the early 1960s, shows large posters both on the Bank and under it. We are exhorted to unzip a banana and encouraged to visit Belle Vue Circus, Leek Horse Fair (the November Hiring Fair) or either of Leek's two cinemas. Anyone with money to spare could attend the Christmas Bazaar to be held in Leek Town Hall. Those were the days!

Left of the Quaker Cottages is Overton Bank House. Many people will remember this property when it was occupied by John Nokes and Sons, cabinet makers. John Nokes ran his business from the Wilkes Yard before moving to Overton Bank. Next to the Swan is the shop where William Laverack Bullock operated for over 30 years as a cabinet maker, now part of JD's wine bar, it was once an early Co-operative Society shop. This photograph also shows the George and the properties in Church Street which have all been demolished.

Choirboys flanked by men in regalia pass Clerk Bank making their way between lines of solemn faced individuals as they process to the church. It has been suggested that this may be the Ancient Order of Buffaloes. If anyone can identify this photograph please contact the authors.

High Street looking over the site of the present car park. Most of the houses have gone. The address of people living in the houses to the left of the photograph was Globe Passage. The only part of this ancient thoroughfare to survive runs from the car park through a cobbled alley to join Salisbury Street.

The house on the left is 4, Clerk Bank which now houses Altered Images, a hair and beauty salon. In the early years of the century it was the home of Isaac Clowes, a boot maker.

The property second from the left was the home of Leek's first Co-operative Shop. It started life here in 1859 but soon moved across the road to 1, Overton Bank a few years later. In 1892 Thomas Cosgrove, a watchmaker lived here before moving to Broad Street.

Chapter 6 - Petty France

The enigmatic character of the cottages behind St. Edward's Church is captured in this evocative photograph. Known locally as Petty France the rows of cottages comprised Ball Lane and the courts leading from it. Petty France is thought to be a corruption of Petite France (Little France) and this area was once believed to be the home of all the French Prisoners who lived in Leek in the early 19th century. Recent research has found that most of these houses were not built until after 1808 and that the prisoners were, in fact, lodged all over the town. Perhaps some Frenchmen did lodge here for a short time but the name Petty France is more likely to have arisen because of the close proximity of the lower churchyard where several of the prisoners are buried. The cottages were demolished in the 1960s and another aspect of Leek's history disappeared for ever.

This row of four cottages faced the wall of the church yard. The shop on the corner was a grocers and sweet shop kept by Mrs. Sharratt.

The same shop is seen on the right and across the lane is St. Edward's Cottage which still stands. Part of the building on the far left was used as a Wesleyan Institute.

This group of three cottages were in a court off Church Lane. *See plan on page 77*

This row of eight terraced cottages was in the court at the bottom of Ball Lane.

Ball Lane leading down to Brough Park with St. Edward's Cottage on the left.

Ladies with shopping bags make their way up the steep slope of Ball Lane on their way into the town. The lane has cobbles only on the left.

Keith Drury walks briskly over the uneven road surface of Ball Lane, without the burden of his postman's bag.

Above (right) and left: Two more views of Ball Lane

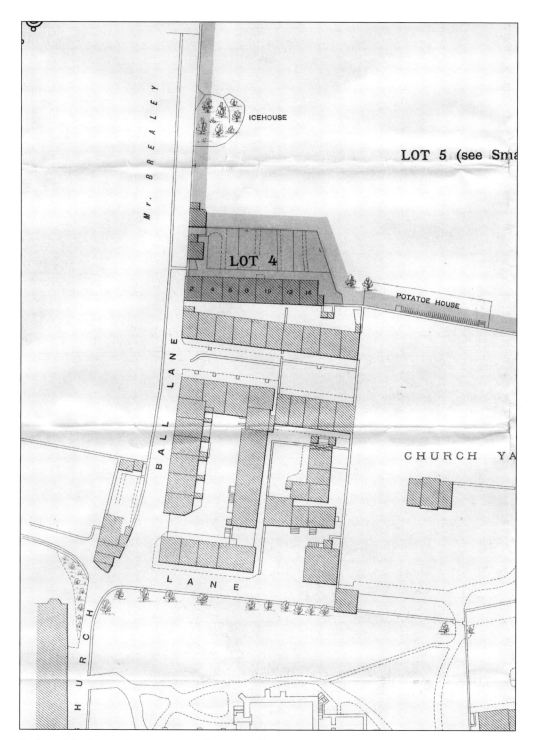

A plan of the houses in Petty France showing Ball Lane and the courts off it. All the houses shown here are included in the preceding photographs. The Icehouse belonged to Mrs Cruso of the house now known as Fowlowe, which she knew as No. 1, Leek. All of this land, where the houses of Petty France once stood, is now part of Brough Park.

Rearguard of the Lancers passing through the town in the mid 1890s. By this time local regiments had purely an overseas military rôle following the establishment of local police forces. The garden in front of Sugden's house at 13, Derby Street can be clearly seen. The shop front of Boots now stands on this garden.

Derby Street on a busy Wednesday. The cobbled road is lined with carrier's carts and the pavement crowded with shoppers. In 1908 the building on the extreme left was used as offices by the Leek Photographic Society, Samuel Mottram, an auctioneer and valuer, and by Mary Nixon a teacher of music. The double fronted property next door housed John Harry Osbourne's butchers shop and the Dog and Partridge public house. On Wednesday's carriers, carts left the Dog and Partridge for Alstonefield, Warslow and Waterhouses.

The same view on a quieter day. The large house, behind the tree, on the left of the photograph is Gaunt House. This was once the home of Richard Gaunt who died in 1844. His daughters, Frances, Louisa, Ellen and Catherine lived in this house for many years after his death. Gaunt House was a substantial property with courts, gardens and pleasure grounds. It was converted into shops, known as Gaunt Buildings.

The proclamation of King George V on May 11th 1910 was an important civic occasion for the people of Leek. Here the civic parade is seen heading along Derby Street towards the Market Place.

William Henry Eaton was a stationer and printer at 6, Derby Street. In 1872 this shop was occupied by James Rider who was also a printer. Mr Rider was a very busy man; he ran the Leek Book Society and the Stamp Office from this shop besides acting as Registrar of births, marriages and deaths for the Leek District. A few years ago, the Moorlands Press was still active, but operating from the Isle of Skye!

James Hall Tatton, baker and confectioner, traded here from at least 1908. He moved to these premises at 22, Derby Street from another shop on the opposite side of the street which later became the Maypole Stores.

J.H.Tatton and Co. was given a false black and white frontage so that it would blend in with the Roebuck Hotel. Many Leek people will remember Tatton's bread with it's distinctive wrappers or recall the ladies who served them coffee and scrumptious cakes. These ladies in their black uniforms with white caps and aprons were required to keep their hair short or fastened up and were not allowed to wear perfume or nail varnish.

The site of Tatton's after it was demolished revealing the side of the Roebuck. A modern building was built here which became Foster's menswear shop. Today this shop trades as Ponden Mill.

On the photograph (below) the public weighing machine has now been replaced by public conveniences. Note the gas lamps lining each side of the street. On the right is 65 Derby Street, the home of Leek's Public Baths for many years. At one time as many as 200 people used the slipper baths for their weekly ablutions. Patrons would wait in a room for their turn to bathe. Females would be conducted to a bath by the superindentent's wife. She filled the bath for you and turned off the hot tap very tightly to stop you getting more than your fair share of hot water! The bath cost 6d and a towel and bar of soap were provided. When stepping out of the bath it was wise to keep an eye out for cockroaches!

(continued below)

Swimmers had the use of the 60 feet by 20 feet white tiled pool. At first, mixed bathing was not allowed but when it was introduced some years later attendances at the baths soared.

The Baths were demolished in 1975 and a new building now stands on the site which is a branch of the Britannia Building Society.

This early view of Derby Street clearly shows Carding's, grocers and corn dealers. Sacks outside the store are most likely waiting to be loaded onto the cart. It later became Biddulph and District Agricultural Society's premises. The shop opposite Carding's was Goldstraws and has subsequently been rebuilt.

To the left can be seen Skinner's shop and Fred Hills. John McPherson Skinner, hardware dealer and ironmonger traded at 62, Derby Street in the early years of the 20th century. Skinner's shop has expanded and now incorporates the premises at 64, Derby Street. Fred Hills bookshop and stationers is now Coffee Beans.

Looking out over Fountain Street towards Derby Street. The large open space in Haywood Street used for the Cattle Market can be clearly seen. Sander's buildings dominate the corner of Derby Street and Haywood Street and the Primitive Methodist Chapel looms large on the left hand side of Fountain Street.

An interesting view of the street taken in the 1950s. Carding's corn store is now Biddulph and District Agricultural Society. H.E. Shingler traded as a tobacconist in the shop in the left foreground. The sign for Brocklehurst's garage can be seen centre left. The garage was off the main street, approached through a passage between shops.

By the time this photograph was taken Brunswick Chapel and the Town Hall have been demolished and Britannia Building Society occupies the site of the Public Baths. Leek United Building Society has replaced the Duke of York and the two shops on the left are trading as Kelly's and Your Pet. They once housed Halfords cycle shop and Deavilles butchers.

A row of shops. From left to right are Knowles (butcher), Brindley (coal merchant), Melias (grocers) Moreton (clock and watchmakers) and the Midlands Electricity shop. In 1912 these same shops were occupied by Messina Knowles (butcher), Sam Brindley (fruiterer), Done (shoe dealer), Moreton (clock and watchmakers) and Moreton (grocer).

Today Bould's butchers has replaced Knowles. Melia's is Strawberry Fields (bakers) and Sketchley (dry cleaners) together with Peak Pharmacy occupy Moreton's old site. The M.E.B is now a charity shop called Scope. Note the large advertisement for Players cigarettes, now definitely taboo!

Houses in Derby Street long since converted to shops. To the left are the arched windows of Bayley's butchers shop. The small house in the centre was supposedly once the home of a Mrs. Bill. The imposing house with six windows was, in 1892, the home of John Brearley. He was born in Leek in 1832 the son of Thomas Brearley, a land agent. By 1871 John Brearley was the senior partner in the Brearley firm of land agents and surveyors. The house on the extreme right was the home, in 1908, of Archibald Somerville M.D. Physician and Surgeon. The conversion from house to shop is recorded in this scene.

The same properties in the 1960's with shops at ground level.

Flags flying to mark a festive occasion in Derby Street. In 1892 the two shops either side of the entrance to Deansgate were, on the left, William Eaton (baker) and on the right, Miss Mary Deane (milliner). A gate used to hang between the properties across Deangate. To the left of Deansgate is a wooden structure. What was its purpose? The glass lantern slide is broken, hence the lines across the photograph.

Pupils from Brunswick Sunday School parade demurely over the cobbles in Derby Street in the 1940s.

Over 30 years separate these two photographs. In the sixties Fine Fare Supermarket stood on the site of the Duke of York. In 1999, 2nd Leek Scouts march past these same shops. Fine Fare has gone, replaced by the Leek United Building Society. Whittaker and Biggs have moved into the premises formerly occupied by the Craft shop with Wright's Pie shop next door. Leading the scout band are Doug Rogers, Matthew Walton and Ian Potts.

The double fronted property to the right of the Duke of York was once Birchall's shops. Mr Anos [sic] Birchall was a hairdresser at 55, Derby Street as early as 1868. By1892, he also occupied the other shop and was trading as a hairdresser and tobacconist. At Birchall's you could choose between three classes of haircut, 1st, 2nd and 3rd. The lather boys would vie to get the 1st class customers as they gave bigger tips! Old Mr. Birchall would cut the hair of gentlemen and mill owners 'by invitation only'. These special haircuts took place at the rear of the premises and involved a convivial glass of whisky shared between client and hairdresser. After many haircuts Mr. Birchall became overly fond of his whisky and would be locked in a bedroom by his relatives to dry out. Strangely, he did not seem to improve which puzzled his family until they discovered him lowering a basket out of his window. The landlord of the adjoining Duke of York was replenishing his supplies which were quickly hauled up to the bedroom!

Morton's Yard. A court off Derby Street reached through an entry next to 42, Derby Street. These houses have now been demolished and the yard is no longer accessible.

A fine team of horses wait patiently for the passengers to board the coach which will take them to Buxton. People crowd the pavement outside the Duke of York waiting to watch the coach move off.

The Duke of York was one of Leek's old public houses. In 1804 Mary Lees, daughter of the landlord, married Jacques Francois Neau. Captain Neau was one of the French Napoleonic prisoners of war who were paroled to Leek. Arriving in Leek in December 1803 he had wooed and married Mary within a few months of his arrival!

Before the Monument was erected this large open space at the east end of Derby Street was used for cattle markets, fairs and numerous entertainments of every kind. The air rang with the cries of cheap-jacks, music and singing accompanied the sales patter of various travelling hawkers. Sequoia the Indian, who sold pills and potions, fascinated small children with his feathers and head-dress. Tobias, a black man, would begin his sales pitch with communal singing, his wife and small boy playing a harmonium.

May and November would see the fairs with their hobbyhorses, gondolers, swingboats, roundabouts and a cakewalk. Gypsy fortune tellers set up their booths and all kinds of treats could be bought from the stalls set up around the square.

A cattle market was held here every fortnight from 1827. The cattle market moved to Haywood street in 1874 when a new Smithfield was built.

The fence on the right marks the boundary of the old cattle market. The house is Cawdry House, later replaced by Cawdry Buildings

Travelling theatres played in the old cattle market area including John Snape's and the Victoria Pavilion Theatre. One of the old 'rag and stick' theatres is pictured here. Rag and stick shows used waggons equipped with canvas sheets (rags) and wooden frames (sticks). The waggons formed the stage while the canvas covered frames sheltered the audience from the weather. They usually played to packed houses and had a variable repertoire.

President Kemp's Palace of Light and Music was another of these travelling theatre companies. To tempt the townspeople to pay to see the show, Kemps had dancing girls who perfomed on a wooden platform erected on the cobblestones. Alice Ralphs remembered watching these dancing girls as a young child, but she never saw the show as she couldn't afford the entrance fee.

Sanders Buildings built for William Sanders to a Sugden design in 1894. With its oriel window, stone pilasters, decorative urns and domed turret the building embraces the Arts and Craft movement which typifies much of Sugden's architecture. In 1896 the two shops were occupied by Mr. Sanders, who was a florist and seedsman and William Mears who traded as an outfitter. Eventually James Mears, nephew of William Sanders took over the florist business so that the Mears family traded from both these shops. They continued to do so for many years and the building became known locally as Mears' Corner. A closer look at this lively photograph will reveal many details, including cows passing in front of the buildings.

A fine view of Sparrow Park, the name given to the area in front of The Monument in the days before traffic began to roar past the roundabout. It was possible to sit beneath the tree and enjoy the peace and quiet!

In the background is the Cattle Market Inn built by Thomas Fernihough in 1867, who also built St. Luke's Church. The Inn gained its pleasing frontages in 1875 when Thomas Brearley enlarged and altered the property, adding moulded bricks, decorative terracotta tiles and carved stonework. The Cattle Market Inn was always popular with both farmers and townsfolk during the hustle and bustle of busy market days.

Deakin's Cooperage traded from 1 and 3
Derby Street for many years. Mr Deakin,
known locally as 'Tub Thumper' Deakin
made barrels, shoulder yokes and other
wooden dairy and agricultural equipment.
It is not known whether the boys posing in
their cloth caps and clogs outside the shop
are family members or passers by.

Mr and Mrs Deakin pictured outside their
shop. This site is now occupied by
Graingers who sell china and glassware.
Between Deakin's and Grainger's these
two shops have in the past housed
Hunter's the teamen, the London Meat
Company and McKellan's opticians.

13, Derby Street. This fine house was the home and offices of the architects William Sugden and Son. In 1881, William lived here with his wife, four adult children, a cook and a housemaid.

13, Derby Street. Sugden's house once had two shops built on the former front garden. In 1908 George Herbert Cousins was a chemist and druggist here. He supplied photographic material of all kinds together with agricultural and patent medicines of every sort. Four years later he added eyesight testing to his services describing it as a speciality. His shop became Timothy Whites and Taylors shop before being taken over by Boots.

13a. Derby Street. Next door was Percy Pickering, a hosier and hatter. He had moved to 1, Gaunt Buildings by 1932.

4, Gaunt Buildings. One of the shops on the ground floor of the former Gaunt House in Derby Street. Armstrong Bros. tailors and clothiers traded here for many years.

7, Derby Street. In 1892 Henry George Carr traded as a linen and woollen draper, silk mercer, hatter, hosier, glover and funeral furnisher. This is now Birthdays card shop.

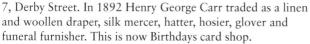

In the early 1900's John Brindley Bayley kept this shop on the corner of Derby Street and Market Street. It is now 'Chapter One' a stationers and booksellers.

John West, an ironmonger traded here at 16, Derby Street from the early 1900s. He had previously worked with Mr Wooliscroft, a few doors away at No. 12.

JOHN WEST,

SPORTS OUTFITTER,

Ironmonger, Implement Agent, Seedsman

Oil and Paint Merchant.

SOLE AGENT FOR

"MELOTTE" CREAM SEPARATORS.

If you want the best Cream Separator you must get the Melotte.

The 1908 Model is the result of 20 years experience and is guaranteed superior to all others.

Beware of Inferior Machines offered at lower prices.

Thousands of Inferior Separators have been sold at scrap iron prices and replaced by Melottes.

LARGEST STOCK OF

SWINTON, HERALD, and other RANGES, PARLOUR GRATES & MANTLE PIECES.

16, Derby St. & Russell St., Leek.

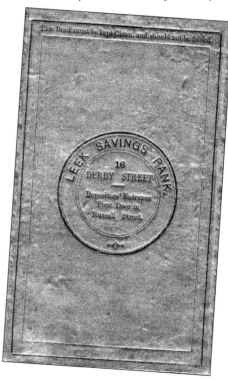

Leek Savings Bank operated from 16, Derby Street in the late 19th century. In 1872 it was only open on Mondays between 12 and 1pm.

27/29 Derby Street.

Charles Kirkham had a draper's shop at No.27 in 1872. A few years later he had taken over No.29 as well. Kirkham's sold books, stationary, music, hosiery, tobacco, fancy pipes and paraffin lamps. As can be seen from the board above his shop Mr Kirkham was also a printer. In 1892 his entry in a directory describes him as a copperplate, lithograph and letterpress printer.

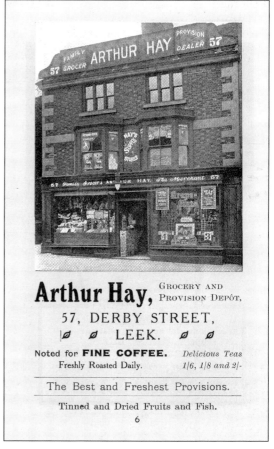

John Fallon's Fruit and Poultry Shop at 14 Derby Street. This later became William Fallon & Co. This building is now occupied by a charity shop which raises money for Cancer Research

Arthur Hay advertised his business in Kelly's Directory in 1912. 57, Derby Street was once occupied by George Mason, who was also a grocer. Today a completely different commodity is sold from this site, it is the home of a branch of Bargain Booze!

The Monument, or more correctly, the Nicholson War Memorial, was unveiled on August 20th 1925. It was built on land owned by the Leek Urban District Council, and the trustees of the Leek Town Lands. Construction had originally been impeded by waterlogged sand. It was so bad that hundreds of cement bags were literally thrown into the huge hole in order to provide a base upon which the structure could be built.

On a fine Thursday, thousands of spectators came to watch the ceremony. The railed off enclosure contained seats for the guests of Sir Arthur and Lady Nicholson, members of Leek UDC and other prominent townspeople. Outside this area space was allotted for the members of the 243rd (Heavy) Battery of the Royal Artillery; the T.A.; the Artillery Band; ex-Servicemen; widows and families of the fallen; plus other groups.

The 243rd (Leek) Battery paraded from the Alma Street Barracks and the National Reserve from Field House in High Street. Members of the Battery stood on each corner of the Monument with arms reversed. They were Bombardiers H Cope, H Nott, H Johnson and Gunner T Thomas. Just over 14 years later, the 2nd World war started and there was a further service on 6th November 1949 to unveil the plaques to those who had died between 1939 and 1945.

Today, The Monument with its inscriptions of Great War Battlefields above the clock, stands proudly in the centre of town. It is appropriate that this huge structure reminds us daily of the sacrifice made by earlier generations of Leek lads in the service of King and Country. Volume 2 of this book will contain a section on the town at war.

The unveiling ceremony (above and below left), plus the programme for the fallen of the 1939-45 conflict.

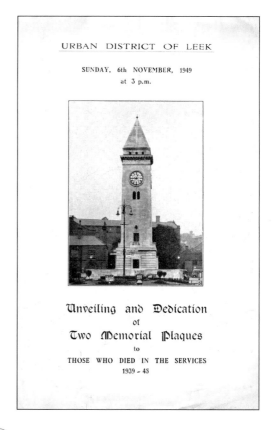

Two different parades in Derby Street. The lower scene looks toward the chimneys of Brough, Nicholson and Hall.

The following photographs (below and opposite) were taken on Club Day in 1961 from outside the new Smithfield Shopping Centre. The bottom photograph shows the banner of Ball Haye Green Methodist Sunday School. In the background are the Bethesda Chapel on the corner of Ball Haye Street and Queen Street, and Raymond Cope's Chemist and Pedley's furniture shop on Fountain Street.

The bottom photograph is believed to show St. Paul's Sunday school children. The Sunday school in the upper photograph has not been identified.

This narrow cobbled passageway connected Derby Street to Brook Street. It started life as Black-a-moor's Head Lane before becoming known as Backsides. Understandably the inhabitants were not overly impressed by this name and asked William Challinor if the name could be changed to Pickwood Road. The following pages comprise a unique photographic record of the houses which once stood in this part of old Leek.

A gas lamp hangs from the wall at the top of Pickwood Road in order to light the narrow, enclosed passageway from Derby Street. This building may be the silk shade, three stories high, which was offered for sale in Black-a Moor's Head Lane in 1834.

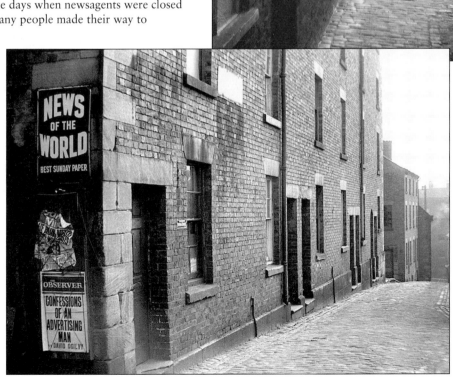

The poster advertising the "News of the World" marks the site of Bloore's wholesale newspaper business. In the days when newsagents were closed on Sundays many people made their way to Pickwood Road to buy their paper from Mr. Bloore. Men and boys would trundle along to the building with little carts which they filled with newspapers to sell around the town.

Small terraced houses with few rooms lined Pickwood Road. The occupants of these houses could easily look over a wall to the large gardens of houses in St. Edward Street. There, ladies would be taking their leisure or indulging in a game of tennis. A marked contrast to the way of life of people who lived in Pickwood Road.

Two ages of a building are shown here, large stone blocks are topped by small regular shaped bricks, probably indicating a rebuilding at some time.

Boarded up windows and broken panes predominate in this view of a desolate and dilapidated Pickwood Road. It was taken in the early 1960s.

This factory was situated at the bottom of Pickwood Road. The houses and premises in Pickwood Road were demolished in 1984 to make way for the new Normid Superstore and its car park. The line of Pickwood Road still remains connecting Brook Street with Derby Street.

Looking down the length of Market Street with Ford House in the left foreground. The garden to the side was originally much larger but was sold off for building land. Nearby Ford Street was built on part of this land. Further along the same side of the street is Brunswick Chapel and on the right hand side is the Town Hall. Both of these properties have been demolished.

Although not of Market Street, these photographs were taken at the same time as the previous one. They show (above) the scene to the east down Stockwell Street and (below) Cruso's Yard.

Roland Tatton and Peggy Starling take the salute outside the Town Hall as guides, led by Mrs. Wright, parade past them. Standing between Peggy and Roland is Harry Hood.

Soldiers stand to attention and bugles ring out as local dignitaries assemble outside the Town Hall in 1910 for the proclamation of King George V.

Looking over at the Town Hall from the site of the demolished Brunswick Chapel. This area is now a neatly laid out car park. The Town Hall started life in 1878 as Union Buildings which was built as a concert hall. Leek Improvement Commissioners purchased these premises in 1881 and the building became the Town Hall. Serving both as the headquarters of the town council and as a venue for leisure and cultural activities in Leek, it provided a service which has not yet been replaced. The Staffordshire Moorlands District Council now operates from new premises off Stockwell Street but the dances, concerts and amateur dramatic performances staged in the large concert hall have not found a satisfactory replacement.

The Town Hall surrounded by scaffolding and with most of its roof gone as it is demolished in 1988.

The Nicholson Clock Tower known locally as The Monument is a memorial to Leek men who gave their lives in the two world wars. It stands on the site of the old cattle market which was held here from 1827. A new Smithfield opened, just round the corner, in Haywood Street in 1874 which was enlarged twenty years later by the addition of the Town Yard in Leonard Street. This view is from the entrance to Talbot Passage, adjacent to the Cattle Market.

A gathering of German Gypsies who came to Leek cattle market in 1906 to take part in the annual horse fair. Photographs exist of them in Ashbourne, in 1906, too.

A foreign visitor shows his horse to best advantage as local fanciers appraise the animal with phlegmatic moorland acumen!

Scenes from the horse fair as horses are put through their paces in front of Cromwell Terrace.

The auctioneer takes charge of the proceedings while sharp eyed buyers in bowler hats examine the goods.

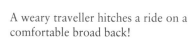

A weary traveller hitches a ride on a comfortable broad back!

A dreary day. Looking towards the cattle market from the bottom of Derby Street. Today the scene looks completely different, apart from the post box which appears to be in the same place.

People wait patiently in the bus shelter while young lads linger to look at the cows. Buses to Cheddleton and the Potteries would often be lined up along Haywood Street to collect their passengers before Leek had a purpose built bus station. This photograph also shows the Talbot Hotel, the Smithfield Commercial Restaurant, and Smithfield Cottages. The Smithfield Restaurant was once the Coffee Tavern which was opened on 12 November 1878, by supporters of the Temperance cause. Their aim was to provide a venue where friends could meet for social recreation instead of frequenting public houses. Working men could bring meals in free of charge rather than eat sitting on the curbstones. Tea, coffee and cocoa were provided before work and soup was available every day at 12 noon. There was a reading room and a place to smoke tobacco and a 'settling room' made available each Wednesday where farmers could sort out their business.

These beasts were probably transported to the market on cattle wagons but in days gone by drovers would collect the cattle from outlying farms and walk them into Leek. Mr. Docksey can remember cattle being collected from Barn Farm at Wetley Rocks every Wednesday at 8am.

Mottrams were one of two auctioneers who operated from the cattle market, the other being J. Oakes Ash. Mottrams would sell until 5pm as they dealt with fat stock, calves and sheep. Ash's finished selling at 3 to 4pm as the dairy cattle they sold would have to get to their new farms in order to be milked.

The cattle market with the shops of Haywood Street in the background. The Co-op sign hangs from the building which now houses Autospares at 63 to 67 Haywood Street. The Co-op shop at 67 was once a hairdressers. Sam Braddock's tonsorial establishment was situated here in the early years of this century followed by James Sigley who also cut hair. By 1932 Edward Grainger, a china dealer had taken over the shop. Eliza Brough's dining rooms once occupied 65, Haywood Street. Tomlinson and Grindey's signboard can be seen over the door of the shop which is now Photoprint. In the early 1900s this was the Telephone Call Office.

This edifice, complete with dome, once stood in Sparrow Park at the end of Derby Street. It is pictured here in Haywood Street where it served as a sweet and tobacconist shop flanked by public conveniences.

The large building here with its wrap-around windows has hardly changed at all but the site opposite is almost unrecognisable. Burgess's Agricultural Showroom has gone, the site was used as a car park for some time, but was transformed by the building of an Aldi supermarket which opened in late August 2000.

On the extreme left of this picture is UFS large walk round store. In 1960, when this photograph was taken, you could buy a 3 piece suite from them for £38.7.6d and an all wool deep pile hearth rug for £2.7.3d. The Co-op electrical showrooms can be seen as can the offices of the Leek Post at 79, Haywood Street. These offices are now part of Genie's which stretches from 75 to 81. Reginald Pointon, a butcher, was at no. 75 in 1912 and Gertrude Broster traded here as a milliner in 1932. Leek Cycle Co. sold bicycles at 81, Haywood Street in the first decade of this century. The former Carriage Restaurant, now Scorpio's take-away, was once home to Marquis Adolphus Cope, a wood carver. George Gunia's jewellers shop was for many years a saddlers shop run by John Henry Shaw.

In 1960 the days of the cattle market were numbered. On this open area the Smithfield Shopping Centre and the Bus Station have been built. When the shopping centre opened a large supermarket called Elmo's occupied this site; it later became Fine Fare and is now Wilkos. Cadman's Electrical Showroom was one of the first businesses to occupy premises in the new Smithfield Centre.

Buses still using Haywood Street to pick up/ drop off customers as the Shopping Centre is being built.

Another view of the Cattle Market. Cars were parked wherever there was a convenient space.

Clearing up after a hard day's work.

Faces full of character belong to Bill Whilock of Hulme Dale Farm in Werrington and Brian Plant.

Two more market day characters!

The last stragglers reluctantly leave the comfort of a wagon to face an uncertain future at the market. The cattle market closed in 1960 moving to a new site off Junction Road. The new market had sections for attested cattle, calves, sheep, pigs, poultry and barren cattle. Enclosures were provided for the sale of farm equipment and 28 business premises were envisaged for shops, offices and banks.

This area of the market was operated by J. Oakes Ash at the bottom of Leonard Street.

Children play happily with hoops on the pavement of Leonard Street. Carts line the street on the left and a quiet and tranquil atmosphere prevails. The house on the left is 10, Leonard Street where Robert Hill had a veterinary practice, the archway has a horses head on top. The next arch, a little further down the street, still has the bottles over it denoting the premises of Richard Massey, ginger beer manufacturer. 'Pop' Massey's cart can be seen outside his factory. The streets in this area of town were named after the owner of the land on which they were built, he was Mr. Leonard Haywood Shoobridge.

Leek's new purpose built Bus Station was officially opened in October 1963. Crowds of spectators watched as a No.49 Jubilee Class single decker, operated by PMT arrived on route from Buxton to Hanley. The station had standings for twelve buses and had the added advantage that passengers would be able to step straight from the buses into the new shopping precinct. The Smithfield shopping precinct was not finished, at this time, but it was planned to build 28 shops and a supermarket. The bus station had a waiting room, an enquiry office and public toilets. It was planned to built a restaurant above the bus station.

Mr. John Else, chairman of the West Midland Traffic Commissioners performed the opening ceremony. He paid tribute to the architect, Mr. Crawford and the Urban Council Surveyor, Mr. J R Johnson. The builders were W H Jones and Sons Ltd. and the designers Shingler Risdon Associates. Messrs. W Zinn were the consulting engineers and Messrs. Harris, Rourke and Simpson the quantity surveyors.

These photographs show the bus station in various stages of construction.

The fairground was held on the site of the Cattle Market in Haywood Street. People are wrapped up against the cold, as this was the November Fair, which evolved from the Hiring Fair, when young people would flock into Leek, hoping to be hired as domestic or farm servants for the coming year.

At dusk the fairground burst into life, with a kaleidoscope of multi-coloured lights, brightly illuminated attractions and booming music. Senses were assailed with the aroma of hot dogs and hamburgers and taste buds activated by temptingly displayed candy floss, toffee apples and popcorn. You could gain a prize by hooking a duck with a winning number, or try your hand at hoop-la. Ping pong balls successfully thrown into glass bowls or buckets would reward you with a goldfish, while skill at darts or rifle shooting provided you with a different trophy!

Further excitement was provided by the gaudily painted rides with their flashing lights and ear-splitting melodies, comprising traditional fairground organ music and pop records. You could take your pick from waltzers, gallopers, dodgems, switchbacks, speedways, chairoplanes or seek new thrills on the Meteorite and the Twist.

The Ghost Train and the Haunted house might scare you, pleasantly, out of your wits, while safer sensations could be found watching the riders on the Wall of Death. Serenely, slipping down the slide of the helter-skelter or crossing a gypsy's palm with silver, the choice was yours. All the fun of the fair was waiting to be found in Haywood Street in November in 1960. Perhaps the earliest reference to the town's November Fair is 2nd November 1594. See *Iron Valley* by H Chester, p.37.

Crossing Cromwell Terrace, a boy with a bicycle and an older gentleman stop to watch the action at the fair. No prizes for guessing which one was looking forward with anticipation and which one was reflecting on the foolhardiness of the people about to climb on to the Meteorite!

One of the popular side shows at the fair, was it Hook-a-Duck or Hoop-la? It was certainly much more interesting than the stall in the background which is practically deserted.

Two of the round-a-bouts provided for youngsters. One had three-a-breast horses and chairplanes while the other provided "a life on the ocean wave" for Leek children. Through the years parents have waited patiently for their children to finish their ride and children eagerly and anxiously have waited for their turn to begin!

A juvenile merry-go-round in all its glory, full of excited children, under a colourful canvas canopy, decorated with cartoon characters.

Speedway or Switchback? Are the two youths waiting for a ride or contemplating the local talent. As always, the dodgems, waltzers and other speedy rides were inevitably used for admiring the opposite sex. A useful aid to romance was the "Caterpillar", which had a collapsible cloth hood which could be raised to cover the riders!

This photograph from the May Fair of 1952 shows a competitor about to take his turn at the Coconut Shy. Hard balls were thrown at coconuts on top of stands, you won a coconut if you could knock them off. Another game, similar to this one, involved throwing at a pile of tin cans, if you succeeded in knocking all of them down you would win a prize.

Another view of the crowded fair on the site of the Cattle Market in Haywood Street.

Michael Collins's transport, carrying the fair rides, parked on the Cattle Market site in Haywood Street. The sweet shop and toilets are no longer with us and although Sugden's scottish baronial style Police Station building still survives, it is no longer used by the forces of law and order.

The Cattle Market where the May and November Fairs were held before transferring to the site of the new Smithfield in Junction Road. In the foreground a woman pushes a pram laden with two children past the bus shelter. The Coffee Tavern and Smithfield Cottages, seen here, have long since disappeared from the Leek street scene.

The Big Wheel soars, high, over the fairground.

Many of the Leek streets were adorned with bunting for the Queen's Coronation in 1953. Several streets also erected decorative arches and many, if not all, of these were photographed by Arthur Goldstraw. The following sequence of photographs record the arches and other scenes in the town at the time. This is Grove Street, with the children of the street gathered together for a group photograph. See page 141 for a further photograph of this arch and Bill Chadwick's shop, which was situated adjacent to it.

The arch by London Mill in Ashbourne Road, showing the procession of the Civic Celebration.

Another view of the Ashbourne Road procession together with properties on the south side of the road including Finikin's Garage.

The reverse view of the Ashbourne Road arch.

The elaborate arch on Buxton Road by Byrne's Garage, close to the Osbourne Street junction. The decorations on Tatton's Mill may also be seen. The gas lamp has long since gone; possibly one of the consignment which went to the USA as antiques.

In 1953 decorations are being erected to celebrate Queen Elizabeth's coronation. A crown adorns the signpost on the roundabout while bunting and flags flutter along the length of the street. To the left can be seen Halford's cycle dealers and Deville's butchers shop. Outside the Duke of York a lorry is parked loaded with beer barrels.

The Public Baths, Birchall's shop, Brunswick Chapel and the Town Hall still stand proudly in the centre of town.

The front of Job White's Mill on Compton and the entrance to the offices proudly decorated with the royal Coat of Arms and a twelve feet high framed portrait of the new monarch.

In addition to the impressive decoration fronting Job White's Mill, Compton has an arch welcoming visitors to Leek. Judging by the adjacent houses, this was a huge structure. Even the gas lamp looks as though it has been repainted for the occasion.

Bunting in Russell Street

The headquarters of Leek United and Midland Building Society in 1953.

The arch on Broad Street.

A deserted Derby Street by Densems on the corner of the Market Place, looking across to Modes (ladies clothes); Cash & Co. (shoes); The Bird in Hand and Bass & Son, the last two with a Union flag.

Grove Street erected its own archway ahead of its street party. Bill Chadwick displays the Coat of Arms and Union Flag above his hardware shop and Grove Street looks full of bunting.

Broad Street at the time of the earlier celebrations in 1936, included for comparison purposes.

Livingstone Street not only put up bunting but also painted its curbstones – presumably red, white and blue – in 1953.

43, Shoebridge Street decorated for the big day. This was the home of Arthur and Alice Goldstraw. The property had previously been an oatcake shop, run by Hannah Simpson.

Stanley & Hope Porter [joint author's parents] purchased their first television from Hammersley's shop in Derby Street to watch the Coronation at home. For many with no TV, other arrangements were necessary. Here a group of people watch the state occasion on TVs in the windows of Hammersley's shop. The news of the first ascent of Everest by a British expedition also broke at the time of the Coronation. Pathe News proudly recorded both items for showing at the town's three cinemas in the following week.

Introduction

Andrew Stacey Turner was born in Mill Street, Leek, in 1895. He was a keen boy scout, joining St. Edward's troop in 1910 and eventually gaining a King's Scout Badge. His life long enthusiasm for the Scout Movement led to him becoming chairman of the Leek and Moorlands Boy Scout Association. After leaving school Andrew became an apprentice bricklayer, working with his father. During the Great War he served in the Royal Army Medical Corp transporting wounded soldiers from the front to the Channel ports. In 1933 he was made a partner in the family firm of W. Turner and Sons who were builders.

Andrew Turner was elected as a councillor for the Leek Urban District Council in 1946 and later served as the chairman of the Baths Committee. In April 1954 he became chairman of the L.U.D.C. The Turner family are fortunate to have a photographic record of Andrew Turner's year of office. Some of these photographs are reproduced in this chapter while others have been included elsewhere in the book.

"Moorview" in Buxton Road was opened as a residential home for old people in 1954, the opening ceremony performed by the Lady Mayoress of Stoke on Trent, Alderman Mrs B. Meakin. In the centre of the group are Mr and Mrs A.S. Turner and Mrs C. Stanford, the matron of the home. By 1976 Moorview had become a children's home.

Leek Salvation Army annual sale of work held at the Citadel in Salisbury Street. Pictured with Andrew Turner, Councillor J.R. Brindley and Captain H.E. Smith are two year old Paul Hudson and Ian Jennings, aged three.

Attending a Garden Party at Knivedon Hall. Edith Turner stands to the right of her husband while their daughter, Audrey, is immediately behind her mother. Standing behind the table is Councillor John Sales. Knivedon Hall, dated 1901, was once the home of Frank Garnet Johnson.

Six hundred pensioners attended the Leek and District Old Age Pensioners Association party at the Town Hall in January 1955. Guests of honour included Captain and Mrs. H.E. Smith of the Salvation Army, Mr. and Mrs. A.S. Turner, Mrs. A. Meakin, Mr. E. (Tiny) Bostock, Councillor Johnson JP and Mrs. Johnson, Mr and Mrs. Valentine, Mr. and Mrs. W. Sharpe and Mr. and Mrs. C. Birch.

Gingerly holding two new born babies are Mr. A. Smith, the Chairman of Cheadle Rural District Council and Mr. A.S. Turner, the Chairman of Leek Urban District Council. This civic visit took place on a Saturday early in January 1955.

One of the duties of all Council chairmen is to visit the sick on Christmas Day. Here Andrew Turner is seen at the Leek Memorial Hospital's party for the patients on Christmas Day. Patients and staff gather round as Andrew shakes the hand of a young man confined to bed.

Mr.Kenneth Griffiths and his orchestra played dance music at the annual N.A.L.G.O Ball held at the Town Hall in February 1955. Many people were unable to attend the Ball due to a sudden snowstorm.

The need for a refreshment pavilion was discussed at the annual dinner of the Leek Park Bowling Club when Andrew Turner presented the trophies in 1954. Standing left to right are Mr E. Dixon, Mr Arthur Goldstraw, Mr J. Barton (secretary), Mr C. Rushton, Mr R. Hollinshead, Mr G.H. Ratcliffe (treasurer), Councillor Mr S.J. Smith, Mr N. Williams and Mr H. Wagstaff. Seated opposite to Andrew is Mr. F. Tunnicliffe.

Hubert Newton, secretary and general manager of the Leek and Moorlands Building Society presented the prizes at the annual Speech Day of Leek College of Further Education. Seated left to right are Mr. R.M. Thompson (Chairman of the Governors), Mrs. H. Newton, Mr. H. Newton and Mr. E. Lansley (Principal).

Officials and delegates at the Bi-monthly conference of North Staffordshire British Legion branches held at the co-operative Hall in 1955. Seated second from left is Mrs. G.M. Nicholson. Andrew Turner is flanked by Dr. Hallowes and Billy Birch.

Glenice Hancock and Beryl Wilshaw from the "Godwin School of Dance, Ballet and Tap", are happily treading the boards in an entertaining dance routine.

Introduction

Leek has a long established tradition of producing amateur entertainment of all kinds. This chapter concentrates on some of the dance and musical productions staged in the town during the 20th century. Just two of Leek's Dance Schools are represented in the following pages. In 1921 our local newspaper reported that "music is fast becoming part and parcel of the daily life of all classes, and our little town, having awakened from the horrible nightmares of war, is giving full proof of its appreciation and love of the divine art". This enjoyment and admiration still exists today even though amateur societies are limited in their choice of venues to stage productions since the Town Hall was demolished in 1988.

During the 20th century many societies flourished providing excellent amateur entertainment, much valued by the people of Leek. They included Leek Amateur Musical Society which staged productions in the Town Hall until 1913 and Leek Amateur Operatic Society, who used the Grand Theatre until 1927. The Grand Theatre and Hippodrome had been built in 1909 by local builder, Sampson Salt. It was used as a cinema and as a venue for travelling theatre productions, as well as providing an alternative to the Town Hall for local amateur societies. All Saints' Amateur Operatic Society performed shows twice a year at the Town Hall from 1932, apart from a break during the years of World War II.

Leek Orchestral Society was wound up due to lack of support in 1926, but it staged joint productions with Leek Choral Society through the 1930's. The present Leek Choral Society was formed in the 1970's by Keith Davis.

Leekensians Amateur Operatic Society began in 1958 and used the Grand Theatre until 1974, before transferring productions to the Town Hall. The "Leekensians" still entertain Leek people, using Trinity Church, in Derby Street, for their performances.

The second volume of the *Spirit of Leek* will hopefully include photographs from local amateur dramatic societies.

Daryl Boote, Anita Cliffe, Hilary Austerberry, Doreen Needham and Margaret Smith, pupils of Gertie Valentine during the '40's. Mrs Valentine ran the Karlton School of Dance and Tap whose rehearsal rooms were in Brunswick School at the bottom of Regent Street. The Karlton Babes performed at the Town Hall in shows entitled *Variety Night*.

Sylvia and Primrose Godwin, sisters who danced in a cabaret act called, appropriately, "The Godwin Sisters". Sylvia Godwin appeared as a dancer in two films, namely, *Latin Quarter* and *I was a Dancer*, and set up the "Godwin School of Dance". Sylvia taught hundreds of Leek children dances ranging from ballet, tap, ballroom and the Hoola! She had her studio in a room in Globe Passage (opposite The Grand) above the premises where Downes' made their famous toffee. The studio moved to the Rugby Club in Strangman Street, where it remained until its closure in the 1980s. *Startime* and *Showtime* featuring the children from the Godwin School of Dance were staged at the Town Hall.

These three photographs feature pupils from the Godwin School of Dance

Sitting on the boy's knees, adorned with tape measures, are Margaret Whitehead and Glenice Hancock.

Showing a leg are Glenice Hancock and Jean Grant Halfpenny

Hoola Hoola girls galore in this tableaux featuring Elaine Winkle, Jean Grant, June Simms, Ann Mellor, Eunice Cantrell, Angela Hill, Moira Machin, Pat Hollinshead, Glenis Hancock and Beryl Foster.

Pupils from the Godwin School of Dance, Ballet and Tap are happily treading the boards in an entertaining dance routine.

These young girls beam with pride as they pose for their spot in the limelight.

The cast of All Saints' Amateur Operatic Society assembled on stage at the Town Hall for their 1962 production of *"Goodnight Vienna"*. This was the Society's 24th production.

Stetsons, bonnets, flounces and frills in a scene from *Oklahoma* at the Town Hall in 1963. Stuart Rane, Dorothy Holmes, Cyril Rowley and Josie Barlow can be seen in this photograph.

The cast of *The Arcadians* the 1965
production by the Leekensians at the
Town Hall.

Fringes, flappers and flannels portray the
era of the Charleston in All Saint's
version of *The Boyfriend* in 1974.
Among the cast were Patricia Rhodes, Ian
Wilson, Barbara Cartlidge, Marilyn
Rushton, Pam Hurst, Kate Burton and
Caroline Whittaker.

A talented cast of 46 performed in *The Vagabond King* at the Town Hall in 1966. This All Saint's show featured Gordon Alcock, whose portrayal of Francois Villon, leader of the vagabonds, was acclaimed in the local press. Gordon Alcock later became a professional entertainer.

A completely different kind of show could also be seen at the Town Hall in 1966. Here the scouts from 2nd Leek Scout Group can be seen in a production number entitled *Sampan*. The Scout Show was an annual event held at the Town Hall from 1960. Scouts, cubs and leaders from the Group sang, danced and featured in comedy sketches every year until the last show held in 1986, sometimes aided and abetted by Girl Guides. The Scout Show was a happy occasion for both audiences and performers and summed up the good humour and camaraderie which existed in this flourishing Scout group.

The scouts and cubs in the 1969 production which included this scene entitled *Freedom*.

The finale of the 1968 Scout Show where the entire cast traditionally sings "We're riding along on the crest of a wave", although quite often the boys would mischievously change the last few words to "the chest of a slave"!

Fiddler On The roof was performed by All Saint's in the autumn of 1975. Recognisable here are Ken Wilshaw, Harold Shenton, Dave Connel and Tony Murphin.

Having a good time in *Fiddler On The Roof* are Alan Poyser, Bett Walker, Kevin Austerberry and Ian Wilson.

The Moorlanders put on pantomimes at the Town Hall for several years. The cast of
Cinderella is seen here in 1976. Hiding in the back row are Alan Hurst and Robert Plant who
were the front and back of the pantomime cow!

A genuine carousel carrying the cast of the Leekensians who staged *Carousel* at the Town Hall
in 1977. Among the cast are Hilary Davis, John Reeves, Pam Hurst and Ian Wilson.

Rose Marie was the 21st anniversary production of the "Leekensians". By this time the society had become well known throughout North Staffordshire for its polished performances. The Leekensians evolved from enthusiasm shown, by two local grammar schools for Gilbert and Sullivan Operas. The schools jointly produced *The Mikado* in 1954 and *Iolanthe* in 1956. Among the many keen performers, who took part in many of the shows are Chris Birch (nee Docksey), Albert Povey, John Reeves, Ian Wilson and Jean Pointon.

A rousing routine from All Saint's *Showboat* in the spring of 1978.

In this 1981 version of *Cinderella* by The Moorlanders, Pam Hurst played 'Cinders", ably supported by two reverend gentlemen. Derek Ormston from All Saint's Church and Derek Palmer, the curate of St.Edward's, portrayed the ugly sisters.

These fledglings pictured with Sheila Plant, in 1982, include Helen Foster, Jane Hurst and Sarah Plant. They appeared in *Mother Goose*, another Moorlanders pantomime.

Serious faces and stately poses as the Leekensians perform *The Mikado* at the Town Hall in 1983.

Pam Hurst, Eileen Burston and Sue Purdy give it all they've got in *Sleeping Beauty* staged by The Moorlanders in 1884.

Gilbert and Sullivan's *Pirates of Penzance*, on stage at the Town Hall circa 1984/5. The Leekensian lady, with the umbrella, is Hilary Davis.

Ian Mills, the choreographer of *Jack and the Beanstalk* can be seen on the right of this photograph. He was a talented pupil of Westwood High School, taking leading roles in school productions and is now a professional. This Moorlanders pantomime was performed in 1984.

Nine years separate these two productions of *Oliver* by All Saints Amateur Operatic Society. The *Street Criers* in the 1976 show were Jill Riley, Pam Hurst and Pam Cotton. Some of the cast singing, *Who will buy* in 1985, have been identified as Nicky Johnson, Margaret Orme, Jo Walton, Pam Cotton, Tony Murphin, Christine Birch, Ruth Latham and Ray Lovatt. Matthew Turner played the part of Oliver.

Joyfully singing in *Oliver* at the Town Hall, in 1985, are Jo Walton, Julia Allen, Pam Hurst and Carol Price.

Smiling faces in the 1987 production of *Camelot*.

The cast and crew of *Camelot*, assembled outside the Town Hall in 1987. This was the last show staged in the Town Hall before it was demolished in 1988. Ian Wilson was the producer, as well as taking the role of Arthur, Jean Pointon played Guinevere and Ian Brereton portrayed Lancelot. This successful production, with spectacular costumes and splendid scenery, marked the end of All Saints' lavish, large scale musicals. From 1932 to 1987, they had performed nearly every year, but without a venue for their productioms were forced to take a final bow.

Centre Stage are carrying on the pantomime tradition with their production of *Dick Whittington* staged at Westwood Road First School in February 2000.

A momentous occasion in any young girl's life was her participation in Leek's Traditional Club Day Festival, locally known as 'walking round day'. Now comprising a procession of Sunday School children, Club Day derived from the time when members of local Friendly Societies walked through the town. Here Kathleen Pickford poses demurely with her 'walking round' basket in the backs of Gaunt Street in the early 1930s.

A cold day in March 1994 as the memorial to the French Prisoners is unveiled in the lower churchyard on 26th March 1996. The ceromony was performed by The Baron Gourgaud, president of the Fondation Napoléon. Television cameras were present on this occasion

David and Sheila Magnier at the launch of *French Connections* in the Arts Club Room in 1995. This book recounts the history of the French Napoleonic prisoners of war who were paroled in Leek in the early 19th Century. David and Sheila are the great-great-great-grandchildren of Pierre Louis Magnier, a French prisoner, who settled in Leek.

A long line of people queued outside Fred Hill's shop in Derby Street to buy Ray Poole's book *Yesterday's Town* on the first day it was on sale in 1988.

Hezekiah Pickford who features in *Images of Edwardian Leek*, a book where Leek people recall their childhoods in the early 1900s. 'Ezek is picture at the launch of the book in 1984 with his great-niece Cathryn Walton.

A bevy of beauties guarded by a sinister looking devil on a carnival float in August 1976.

Blowing their own trumpets are members of St. Mary's Scout and Guide Band!

The young ladies of St. Luke's choir assembled in the Market Place in the early 1960s. Among this group are Christine Evans and Margaret Hall.

Guides make their way into church on Thinking Day

A gathering of guides at Beechfields in Leek. **Back row.** Sybil Worthington, Dorothy Nettel, Rita Price, Marion Binns, Mrs. Peter Johnson, Muriel Carr, Peggy Starling and Mrs. Oultram. **Middle Row.** Sue Pollock, Patsy Wilson, Eileen Rutter, Jill Griffiths, Janet Sales, Kristine Bell, Megan Griffiths and Margaret Bailey,?,?. The names of the young ladies on the front row are not all known.

Part of the fair in the Market Place which formed part of the Pied Poudre celebrations in the 1970s.

Performers in the castle which was erected at the bottom of Derby Street.

The Lord of the Manor (George Walton) proceeds majestically along Derby Street at the court of Pied Poudre in the early 1980s.

Mrs. Nicholson receiving a presentation from the ladies of the Royal British Legion Womens Section in the 1960s.

Leek Young Conservatives enjoy a social occasion at the Swan c1966.

Front Row. June Beech, Averil Brown, Jane Wilshaw, Cathryn Beech, Michael Fisher and Miss Podmore. Among others pictured are Paul Le Rue, Carol Millington, Stuart Emery and Angela Heath.

Leek District Midwives. Elaine Clowes from the County Council receives a bouquet of flowers, to her left is Mrs. Hill the District Nursing Officer. Between these two ladies is Sister Phyllis Steele, a popular Leek midwife, who delivered multitudes of Leek babies!

The Arts Club Ball at the Town Hall in 1957. Who can spot John Myatt, Roger Pedley, Rowena Hill, Dorothy Newall, Margaret Galley, Della Parker, Heather Berrisford and Hilda Whalley?

Members of Leek Gun Club dine out with their wives and girl friends at the Fox Hotel, Rushton Spencer in the 1970s. Pictured here are Bill and Doreen Salt, Phil Daniels, John Walton, Wendy Lees, Robert Plant, Ken and Audrey Salt and Colin Hargreaves.

Brownies from Wallbridge 12th Leek Group scantily clad in Harem costumes as they prepare to take part in 4th Leek's Scouts Carnival in the 1970s.

The same Brownie group dressed for another carnival occasion

1955. Leek and Moorland Boy Scouts Association held their annual swimming gala at the old baths in Derby Street. The young ladies present must be Guides!

21 July 1958. Participants in the Leek Youth Clubs Swimming Gala at the Derby Street Baths. The Leek and District Girl Guides team won the cup on this occasion.

The Brownie Revels held on St. Edward's Sports Field in 1971.

Cubs and Scouts taking part in a sports day on the Birchall playing fields in 1955.

Boys and leaders from 2nd Leek Scout Group pictured outside their headquarters on Clerk Bank in 1993.
This photograph was taken to mark the 75th anniversary of the foundation of the troop.

The bottom room in Trinity Church before alterations took place. The date is 8th October 1960 and the brownies are having a get together.

St. Mary's Guides march behind their flag in St. Edward Street. The occasion is Club Day but the date is not known.

Happy, smiling faces of a crowd of people gathered outside Leek Railway Station. Are they looking forward to their trip or have they just returned from an enjoyable outing?

Pictured at Coventry Cathedral in 1946 are members of Leek Textile Society. Kneeling second from the left is Harry Hall.

Employees of Haywood Mills are having a good time at their first dance held in the Co-Operative Hall in 1948.

The Moonglows, a talented Leek group, who played at the Top Rank in Hanley during the 1960s. A bus would leave Leek Market Place each Saturday night crowded with girls in mini skirts, stiletto heels and mock Mary Quant clothes. After an evening of hectic Rock and Roll, interspersed with the *March of the Mods* and the *Gay Gordons*, the bus would return them safely back to Leek. That's if they hadn't been offered a lift in the meantime!

Ladies from the Lux Lux design room enjoy a Christmas dinner at the Jester in 1976. (top row from left) Margaret Oliver, Rowena Lovatt, Ann Haime, Shirley Alkins, Joan Baddeley, Gillian Hambleton, Mary Emery (sitting down from left) Mavis Smith, Hope Porter, Barbara Macdonald, Anne Osborne, Rose Howell, Olwyn Chadwick.

Job White's representatives ready to enjoy dinner with their wives at the Southbank Hotel.

Lucinda Lampton interviews stall holders in the Buttermarket for her television programme,

Protesters outside Moorlands House in Stockwell Street. The Staffordshire Moorlands District Council, in 1986, wished to redevelop Leek town centre in order to build a modern shopping precinct behind the Market Place. The people of Leek were not happy, petitions were signed, protests made and the scheme was eventually abandoned. The Ratepayer's Group who opposed this redevelopment were elected onto the council for the first time, at the next local election.

Children performing a Nativity Play in the Arts Club Room in the 1950s.

The Children's section of Leek Library in the 1950s in the basement of the Nicholson Institute.

Miss Jerram the Leek librarian and colleages at the Nicholson Institute.

Playing with a train set in the library tent at Leek Show, 1970.

Pictured outside the library tent at Leek Show on 9th August 1970 are Beryl Hine, Barbara Gould and Margaret Trythall. Miss Edith Jerram is the one **not** wearing a mini-dress.

Mrs Marian Hill presents the trophy for the best W.I. display at Leek Show in 1980.

Making Christmas crackers for the children of Springfield Road School are ladies from the British Legion Womens Section. Pictured here are Margaret Taylor, Marjorie Sherratt, Alice Pickford, Ida Maloney, Ethel Forrester, Connie Vigrass, Ida Shenton and Triss Biddulph among others.

Chief Superintendent Eric Lees and his wife are presented with gifts on the occasion of his retirement from the Police Force in 1978.

Club Day 2000

The final section of this book looks at the last Club Day of the old millennium, in the summer of 2000. Here, participants and the onlookers gather in the Market Place (above) and the band leads off down Stockwell Street.

Six more scenes of the procession proceeding down Stockwell Street.

Index

A
Adam's Yard 9
All Saints' Amateur Operatic
  Society 149
Angel, the 11
Arts Club Ball 173
Ashbourne Road 134

B
Ball Haye Green Methodist
  Sunday School 104
Ball Lane 74
Bethesda Chapel 104
Bird in Hand 9
Black-a Moor's Head Lane
  107
Blacks Head 8
Brickbank 53
Britannia Mill 33
British Legion 148
Broad Street 140
Brow Hill House 69
Brownie Revels 176
Brunswick Chapel 86
Brunswick Sunday School 89
Bull's Head, The 33
Bus Station 114
Buttermarket 11, 182
Buxton Road 135
Byrne's Garage 135

C
Carding's shop 20
Cattle Market 114
Cattle Market Inn, The 95
Cavendish Square 44
Cawdry House 93
Challinor Fountain 7
Church Lane 74
Church Street 57
Clerk Bank 66
Club Day 104
Cock Inn 20
Coffee Tavern 117
Conservative Club 57
Coronation Arches 133
Cottage Hospital 55
Cromwell Terrace 116
Cruso's Yard 43

D
Deangate 89
Derby Street 78
Dog and Partridge 80
Duke of York 91

F
Fallon's 40

Ford House 46
Foxlowe 11
Freeman, Hardy and Willis 11

G
Garden Bank 52
Gaunt House 80
George Hotel 31
German Gypsies 115
Globe Passage 71
Godwin School of Dance 149
Golden Lion 61
Grand Theatre 149
Grapes, The 34
Greystones 48
Grove Street 141
Guide Band 169
Guides 170

H
Haworth's 42
Haywood Mills 180
Haywood Street 119
Hiring Fair 126
Hubert Newton 148

J
Job White's Mill 138
John Naden 20
John West 99

K
Karlton School of Dance 150
Knivedon Hall 145

L
Leek Amateur Musical
  Society 149
Leek Amateur Operatic
  Society 149
Leek and Moorland Boy
  Scouts Association 175
Leek and Moorlands
  Building Soci 44
Leek Bank 43
Leek Book Society 81
Leek Choral Society 149
Leek District Midwives 172
Leek Embroidery Society 33
Leek Gun Club 173
Leek Library 183
Leek Memorial Hospital's
  146
Leek Old Hall 11
Leek Orchestral Society 149
Leek Park Bowling Club 147
Leek Salvation Army 145
Leek Savings Bank 99

Leek Scout band, 2nd 65
Leek Show 185
Leek Textile Society 179
Leek United and Midland
  Building Society 139
Leek Young Conservatives
  172
Leek Youth Clubs Swimming
  Gala 175
Leekensians Amateur
  Operatic Society 149
Leonard Street 124
Livingstone Street 142
Lux Lux 181

M
Majestic Cinema 51
Market Place 7
Market Street 110
Maskery's bakers 34
Monument, The 95
Moonglows, The 180
Moorlanders, The 158
Moorview 145
Morton's Yard 91
Mount Pleasant Chapel 69

N
N.A.L.G.O Ball 147
New Stockwell House 46
Nicholson Institute 48
North Staffordshire Hunt 56
November Fair 126

O
Old Age Pensioners
  Association 146
Old Cheshire Cheese Inn 36
Overton Bank 66
Overton Bank House 67, 70

P
Parker House 59
Parr's bank 36
Petty France 72
Pickford's grocers shop 35
Pickwood Road 106
Pied Poudre celebrations 171
Post Office 37
President Kemp's Palace 94
Primitive Methodist Chapel
  85
Public Baths 83
Public Hall 19

Q
Quaker cottages 70

R
Ratepayer's Group, The 182
Ray Poole 168
Red Lion 8
Roebuck, the 82
Royal British Legion
  Womens Section 172
Russell Street 139

S
Sanders Buildings 95
Shirley's Buildings 35
Shoebridge Street 142
Smithfield Cottages 117
Smithfield shopping precinct
  125
Sparrow Park 95
Springfield Road School 186
St Edward Street 31
St. Edward's Cottage 73
St. Luke's choir 169
St. Mary's Guides 178
St. Mary's Scout 169
St. Paul's Sunday school
  children 105
Star Tea Co 11
Stephen Goodwin and
  Tatton Ltd 68
Stockwell House 45
Stockwell Street 41
Sugden and Son 97

T
Tatton and Co. 82
Town Hall 86
Trades Demonstration 32
Trafford, butchers 16
Treading the Boards 149
Trinity Church 178
'Tub Thumper' Deakin 96

U
Union, the 52

V
Victoria Buildings 32

W
W.I. 185
Wallbridge 12th Leek Group
  174
Wardle, Thomas 38
West Street Sunday School 67
Westminster Bank 36
Westwood Road First School
  165
White Hart 42
Wilkes' Head 36
Woolworths 8

Subscribers List

Mrs M Boys-Adams, Sparkwell, Devon
Mrs DC Ball, Blackshaw Moor
Mrs E Barks, Leek
Mrs JM Bennett, Leek
Mrs Biddulph, Leek
Michael Birch, Leek
Mr Birchall, Leek
Mr GJ Bloore, Leek
Bookthrift, Ashbourne
Bookthrift, Macclesfield
Colin Bowyer, Leek
Kenneth Bowyer, Leek
Mrs DE Brentnall, Leek
Janet Broome, Leek
Brian Brookes, Leek
DB Brookes, Leek
John Brough, Leek
Roger S Burgess, Leek
Janet Burrows, Leek

Mr S Callear, Leek
Chapter One, Leek
Chris Clark, Leek
Ray & Carolyn Cork, Ashbourne

Derby County Library Service
Mrs M Deaville, Lichfield

Valerie Emery, Leek

Ralph Fleming, Leek
Raymond Fletcher, Leek
David & Beverley Foster, Leek

Bob Gratton, Dronfield

Pamela Hurst, Leek
Marian Hulme, Leek

J and J Irish, Leek

Mrs Joan Jones, Leek

Mrs A Keates, Leek
George Keates, Leek

M A Lovatt, Leek

Mrs E J McGrath, Leek

John Newall, Leek

Mr JA Pickford, Endon
Picture Book, Leek
Potteries Museum, Hanley

David Rhead, Leek
Mr B Rushton, Harrogate
Judith C Rider, Leek
J Robinson, Endon

Tony Smith, Leek
Ron Scholes, Leek
Mrs F M Shatwell, Leek
Staffordshire Moorlands Tourist
    Information Centre
K Stonehewer, Cheltenham
P Starling, Leek
Ian Swarbrooke, Leek
Mr F R Stubbs, Endon

The Village Bookshop, Milton
Basil Turner, Leek
Kathleen Turner, Leek

Jonathan and Trudi Walton Leek
Wendy Walton, Leek
Janet & Roger Warrillow, Leek
John White, Leek
Kathleen Williamson, Leek

LANDMARK COLLECTOR'S LIBRARY

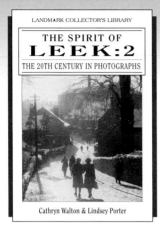
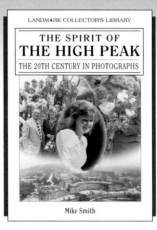
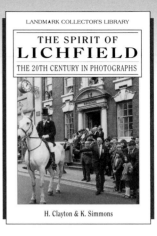
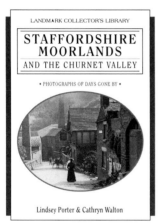
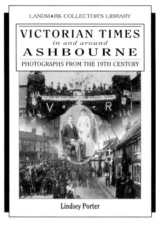
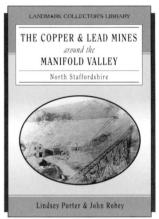